Hidden

Manna

Devotionals by

Dr. Charles W. Shepson

Cover photo by: Wesley Beeler

The bread was baked by Elaine's dear friend, Gloria Stumbo.

The Royal Albert dishes, Old Country Roses pattern, are from
Elaine's set of English bone china.

Unless otherwise noted, scripture quotations in this book are
from the HOLY BIBLE, NEW INTERNATIONAL VERSION,
copyright 1973, 1978, and 1984 by International Bible Society.

ISBN: 1-885729-06-5

Printed by:
Toccoa Falls College Press
Toccoa Falls, GA 30598

Dedication

To the darling of my heart...
   who throughout her life consistently
      ...loved her Lord deeply,
      ...served her Lord faithfully,
      ...enjoyed her Lord's fellowship immensely.

For forty of those years...
   the very same things could be said
      of her relationship to me.

I love her for that,
   more than I could ever express!

Introduction

HIDDEN MANNA is not for everyone! It is not even for all who are experiencing a severe trial. Perhaps an explanation of how this book came into existence will help you determine if it is for you, or for those persons to whom you are thinking of making a gift of HIDDEN MANNA so as to encourage them.

Though the word "cancer" is seldom found in the text, these devotionals were prompted as an aftermath of a traumatic diagnosis of cancer in Elaine's body. That one word shattered our dreams of a beautiful retirement together following a most enjoyable life of service to the Lord, and a marriage that was exceptionally harmonious. It became my firm determination to minister fully to my sweetheart's every need, gladly keeping the promises I had made to her at the altar nearly forty years earlier. Those promises had included the words "worse" and "sickness" as well as "better" and "health." I had meant every word of them.

Ministering to my honey's physical needs, though at times difficult, was fairly readily mastered. Ministering to her spiritual needs proved to be a greater challenge. I could find no book of devotionals that understood how deeply we were <u>both</u> suffering. So, ... I determined to write a devotional each morning to read to her that same evening. I asked God to give me something fresh and encouraging for her daily - <u>and He did</u>!

There would have been 180 or less of these if the predictions of Hospice and our oncologists had been accurate. <u>But I have 400 of them</u>! The chapters of this book include only one out of every four that I wrote for Elaine.

I said that HIDDEN MANNA is not for everyone. True! It is not for persons who don't yet really know Jesus Christ and have not made a sincere commitment of their lives to Him. God's wonderful promises do not apply to them. These devotionals may even prove unsuitable for those whose relationship to Christ has been shallow. The "ark" which Elaine and I wearily climbed into was not hastily constructed. It was a sturdy ship painstakingly assembled over the years.

On the other hand, for the caretaker who desires to provide spiritual encouragement to a spouse, a close friend, or a relative whose situation apart from God is pretty bleak, HIDDEN MANNA may be just what the Doctor ordered. The Doctor I refer to is Jehovah-Rapha (The Lord, your Physician). I send this manuscript off to the publisher with precisely that prayer.

If these devotionals can bring shafts of light into your dark days, ministering to you the way they did to me and to the darling of my heart, I will feel a deep satisfaction in knowing that God has used her pain and my pen to accomplish His purpose.

Note: Whenever an asterisk (*) appears in these devotionals, please reread the opening scripture.

Also note: For the caretaker who is serious about desiring to maximize the spiritual encouragement, I suggest that you read the devotional beforehand and edit it where necessary to fit your circumstances. You may even wish to skip to the next one if the devotional seems inappropriate for what your day has been like. I wrote them very specifically for <u>my</u> sweetheart. I suggest you edit them specifically for <u>your</u> loved one.

HIDDEN MANNA

"To him who overcomes, I will give some of the <u>hidden</u> <u>manna</u>."   Revelation 2:17b

"Hidden manna!" Have you ever heard of that before? Isn't it fascinating to realize that there <u>is</u> a hidden manna stashed away somewhere especially for those who overcome?

God has provided this hidden manna. If we look this verse up in the Eight Translation New Testament we find that all eight of the translations and paraphrases use the term "hidden manna." Only one elaborates. That is the Living Bible, which interjects following the promise of "hidden manna" the words, "the secret nourishment from heaven."

We need that secret nourishment from heaven these days and should be thrilled to discover that God has special thoughts for those who are specially suffering. There <u>is</u> a daily provision laid out for His children to sustain them that comes directly from heaven to the hungry and hurting heart.

This hidden manna is a wonderful gift to the overcomer. God will help us in the midst of the most difficult trial of our lives to be true overcomers. That is pleasing to Him, we know, and we want to be enabled by Him to be in that select regiment called "overcomers" so that we may also enjoy the unique food He has promised to the overcomer: "hidden manna."

The manna God divinely placed upon the ground for the Israelites during their wilderness experience had everything in it they needed to sustain vigorous life. It was placed there faithfully, but God expected them to go gather it faithfully, too. He has provided all we need for each new day as we walk together through this dark, difficult valley. We must be faithful to gather our daily supply of hidden manna so we can stay strong and healthy in spirit.

"To him who overcomes, I will give some of the hidden manna."

HIDDEN MANNA II

"To him who overcomes, I will give some of
the <u>hidden</u> <u>manna</u>."   Revelation 2:17b

Yesterday's serendipity must linger with us. We must recall repeatedly the words "hidden manna." Remember what the Lord Jesus said when the disciples brought meat from the village, arriving right after he had finished witnessing to the Samaritan woman whose heart was open? He said, "I have food to eat that you know nothing about." (John 4:32) That statement must have impressed young John deeply, for he is the only one of the four Gospel writers who mentions the incident, though all of them were there. Apparently he was intrigued by that statement, too. What is this "<u>hidden</u> <u>manna</u>"? Is it the grace God gives to endure? He links the receiving of it with being an overcomer. We have certainly experienced His grace during these days of being laid aside. Each new day there seems to be a new supply of grace, and our spirits do not languish, even while circumstances dictate removal from the spheres of activity we used to know.

Is it the heart strength spoken of by Asaph in the 73rd Psalm where he insists that, "My flesh and my heart may fail, but God is <u>the strength of my heart</u> and my portion forever"?

Is it the quiet reassurance that "God knows the way that we take, and when we are come out of this we shall be as gold" that sweeps over us day after day, and permits a contentment that is unexpected?

Or is it a mystical provision that cannot be analyzed or examined, but is sweet to taste and enjoy, just like the original manna?

We don't know a lot about this "hidden manna" except that it is there for us, freshly prepared and newly offered each morning. A fresh supply for each new day is offered to us and we must gladly accept it, with heartfelt thanksgiving.

"To him who overcomes, I will give some of the hidden manna."

JEDIDIAH

"The LORD loved him; and because the LORD loved him, he sent word through Nathan the prophet to name him Jedidiah."   II Samuel 12::25

> footnote: *Jedidiah* means *loved by the LORD.*

Through this passage the Lord reminds us that He loves His children deeply. He loves <u>you and me</u> deeply, and expresses that love in so many different ways. This verse tells us about a very unusual way that God expressed His love. He named the new baby Jedidiah.

There is a sad sequel to this event, though. No one seems ever to have called little Jedidiah by the name God gave him. We know him as Solomon. That name was given to him by his parents, David and Bathsheba, before God renamed him. Unfortunately, theirs was the name that stuck, ...or is that unfortunate? Maybe his name, Jedidiah, is in the same category as the names God plans to give you and me referred to in Revelation 2:17. That name is to be known only to God and to us.

It is comforting to know that we are very personally known by God and very deeply loved by Him. His love is demonstrated in a variety of ways to each of us. Sometimes that expression of love is generic, as when we quote a verse of scripture that is a blessing to hundreds of thousands of others, as well as to us. Sometimes it is anything but generic, as when God steps into our lives in a serendipitous manner and does something <u>so</u> personal and <u>so</u> sweet that it is comparable to naming a new baby.

No matter what our tomorrow is like, we can bask in the light of the truth that our God loves us - loves us very deeply. He knows when we are desperate for a ray of sunshine, and He is always faithful to let it shine through, even in our darkest hours.

"The LORD loved him; and because the LORD loved him, he sent word through Nathan the prophet to name him Jedidiah."

A NEW NAME

"To him who overcomes ... I will also give a new name, known only to him who receives it." *(in addition to the "hidden manna")*   Revelation 2:17c

There is something exciting about this promise. We are to have new names! But those new names will not be used by others. They will be names only our Heavenly Father will know. There is something deeply intimate and wondrously special about that.

Our earthly names were given to us by our parents, and sometimes modified by family or friends. Rarely in life have we been given a name that only one person uses. Spouses sometimes call each other "honey" or "sweetheart" or some other familiar term of endearment. They may even have a private name that sounds too silly to expose to others, so it is used only when they are alone. Now we are told that our God is going to give us names that only He and we will know. What might those names be?

In Bible times God renamed people, but the difference

then was that it was a new name everyone was to use, having a meaning that described the person. Simon was renamed Peter, or "rock," with deep significance to the renaming. Saul was given the new name Paul, in part to signify the radical change that had come in his life. The renaming was often a dramatic experience.

This new name goes beyond that. It will be a very special name that we will treasure. It will probably reflect what God sees in us and loves in us. It will differentiate us from all other persons in Heaven and will probably stir our emotions deeply when God uses it. What an exciting prospect! Let's be overcomers who eagerly await the receiving of our new names. Let's weather this storm together in a manner that will greatly please God, and even affect the secret name He will give to each of us that wonderful day.

"To him who overcomes ... I will also give a new name, known only to him who receives it."

A DEEP WATER CATCH

"When He had finished speaking, He said to Simon, 'Put out into <u>deep water</u>, and let down the nets for a catch.'"

Luke 5:4

Deep water scares poor swimmers. Deep water has been the undoing of some really good swimmers, too. Yet here the Lord is telling Peter to head for deep water and <u>there</u> He gives to him a tremendous catch that nearly sinks his boat.

How sad when the depth of the water is all that is considered! Deep water has the potential for a phenomenal catch, as well. When its possibilities are ignored, only fear is produced. That truth must be kept in the front of our minds so that we will not be overwhelmed by depth or waves. We must dare to let down our nets as the Master has ordered, finding unbelievably great quantities of grace, of strength, and of peace, even in the midst of our deep water trial. One of Simon Peter's most memorable catches came from deep water. That can happen for us, too.

"Lord, keep me trusting Thee day after day,
  Trusting whatever befall on my way.
    Sunshine or shadow, I take them from Thee,
    Knowing Thy grace is sufficient for me.

  Trusting Thee more, trusting Thee more;
    May every day find me trusting Thee more.
      Cares may surround me and clouds hover o'er,
        But keep me, Lord Jesus,
          Still trusting Thee more."

That kind of trust, even in deep water - no, <u>especially</u> in deep water - will produce a bountiful harvest of all we have need of. Our nets will be full. Our ships will be heaped with a "catch" they can scarcely handle! I wonder what kind of fish <u>they</u> caught? I know what the names of some of the "fish" <u>we</u> catch are: grace, peace, strength, trust, hope, faith, patience (and some of those fish are rarer than others). *

MAKE AN ARK!

"So make yourself an ark ..."

Genesis 6:14a

"Noah, in the light of the troubles that are ahead for you, make yourself an ark," is God's command.

The wise Christian will prepare for <u>bad</u> times when things are going <u>well</u>, remembering that his Lord has told him that "in the world you <u>shall</u> have tribulation." Most people do not thoroughly prepare for anything: retirement, rainy days, old age, sickness, or anything else. That's sad!

<u>Preparations can include Scripture memorization</u>. How often has a memorized verse surfaced in our minds just when it was needed! God loves to speak through His precious Word. When we have committed a verse to memory, the Holy Spirit can easily bring it to the forefront of our consciousness and use it to lift us up so wondrously.

<u>Preparations can include developing choice friendships</u>. We are being sustained in part by the beautiful

expressions of love that come to us regularly from great friends we have come to know and love. We have <u>so many</u> people who write or phone to say that they pray for us <u>every day</u>. That amazes us!

<u>Preparations can include keeping Heaven and earth in perspective</u>. "This world is <u>not</u> my home, I'm just a passin' through. My treasures are laid up somewhere beyond the blue." That's a beautiful truth, not just a lively gospel song. Our earth experience is a very brief prelude to an eternity of joy in the presence of our Savior.

Through the years we have been building an ark without realizing it, plank by plank, nail by nail, and now that the torrential rains have come, we may go into it and find shelter while we ride out this unprecedented storm.

"So make yourself an ark ..."

HOPE FOR YOUR FUTURE

"... 'there is hope for your future,' declares the LORD."

Jeremiah 31:17

This is a six-word promise we must cling to in these days when our <u>only</u> hope for the future is found in the Lord. When we say our <u>only</u> hope is in the Lord, it is sometimes meant to convey how bad things are. We must be careful to recognize that this coin of truth has a very beautiful, shiny side, as well.

When we get down to the point where our <u>only</u> hope is in the Lord, it is well for us to remember that we are very far from being poverty stricken in the hope account! Quite the opposite is true; the hope He provides is a living hope with a firm foundation. It is really <u>all</u> we have need of.

When the Lord says, "There is hope for your future," we need to hold on to that promise tenaciously, believing the best we can. He will add to our feeble faith what is needed to bring the deliverance and triumph He had in mind all along.

"When we have exhausted our hoarded resources, our Father's full giving is only begun." We must apply that principle to hope, and refuse to <u>stop</u> hoping, <u>ever</u>. We know that hope can be interpreted by scientifically-minded doctors as denial. We do not see it that way. We aren't denying anything except their ability to predict accurately. God has the final say about our length of days, and we are quite immortal until our life's work is complete. Many of the earlier predictions of our doctors have not come to pass, thankfully. God has countermanded them by His own edict. Medical personnel should be very careful to qualify any prognosis they make about one of the Lord's children! We are different. We come under a different set of rules! "There is hope for your future" - what wonderful words! How very comforting and reassuring they are!

"... 'there is hope for your future,' declares the LORD."

HE IS THE PLACE TO GO

"The Lord is good. When trouble comes, <u>He is the place to go</u>! And He knows everyone who trusts in Him!"

Nahum 1:7 (L.B.)

How simply this is expressed! And how wonderfully true it is, as well! When troubles come, He is indeed the place to go. And what a comfort to be reminded that "He knows everyone who trusts in Him!"

We are especially blessed to be Christians. There are people who have the same battle to fight, but they do not have the same resources. They are totally dependent upon their doctors, upon the very limited knowledge of this disease that those doctors have, and upon their own will to fight.

We have no such limitations. We have fabulous promises made by One who has proven Himself faithful throughout our lives. We have a Physician whose skills are legendary! He knows things that most physicians know nothing about. He calls Himself Jehovah-Rapha, "The Lord Who Heals;" "The

Lord, Your Physician." He healed all who came to Him when He was walking this earth in a human body. He used His disciples both in Bible times and in every subsequent century to heal thousands. He has responded time after time to the individual's prayer of faith.

We have the elders of the church to come and anoint. We have praying friends with whom praying is not whispering something uncomfortably to "the Man Upstairs;" praying friends with whom prayer is a manner of life.

We have the Lord placing you upon the hearts of people for prayer to the extent that there are people praying for you who have never even met you!

Oh, yes indeed, *"The Lord is good. When trouble comes, He is the place to go! And He knows everyone who trusts in Him!"*

GOD'S FOOTPRINTS

"... though Your footprints were <u>not</u> seen, You led Your people ..."   Psalm 77:19c,20

The poem "Footprints in the Sand" is both famous and impressive. In that imaginary scene the writer comes to understand that God's footprints were <u>always</u> there, even when the sand recorded only one set of them. He was at that point carrying His child! But <u>this</u> picture is a different one. The image here is also one of sand that has only one set of footprints, but this time they are our own and <u>not</u> God's. It is a reminder that there are times in life when God's people have no visible evidence of His Presence, but that the inability to see a set of Divine footprints does not change a thing. <u>He is still there</u>, and He is still leading. <u>Faith tells us so</u>!

We would never say that God's footprints were nowhere to be seen in this dark valley through which He has been leading us. In spite of the darkness, we <u>can</u> see them faintly, <u>and sometimes even clearly</u>!

John Peterson expressed it well when he penned the words:

> "Jesus led me all the way,
>> Led me step by step each day;
>>> I will tell the saints and angels
>>> As I lay my burdens down,
>>>> 'Jesus led me all the way.'"

One of the verses of that song insists:

> "If God should let me there review
>> The winding paths of earth I knew,
>>> It would be proven clear and true -
>>> Jesus led me all the way."

Yes, even when God's footprints are <u>not</u> seen, He is still leading His people. The darkness can totally obscure the sight of His footprints, but it <u>cannot</u> erase His Presence. He has chosen to make His Presence <u>felt</u> rather than <u>seen</u>, and there is infinite wisdom in that decision. *"... though Your footprints were <u>not</u> seen, You led Your people ..."*

FULLY COMMITTED

"... Asa's heart was <u>fully committed</u> to the LORD all his life."   I Kings 15:14b

We want this to be said of us, too, no matter what lies ahead.   If it is complete healing with all its accompanying joys, we want that health and strength to be fully committed to the Lord.   If our future involves pain and suffering, we want no less in the way of total commitment.

Surely God will enable us to live wholly for Him, whichever takes place, for He delights in those who are fully committed, and turns His face toward those who walk before Him in that manner.

It is not always easy to maintain a spiritual stance in the midst of pain and reverses; that requires added grace.   But Annie Johnson Flint was right on target when she penned the words:

"He giveth more grace when the burdens grow greater;
  He sendeth more strength when the labors increase.
   To added affliction He addeth His mercy;
    To multiplied trials, His multiplied peace.
 When we have exhausted our store of endurance,
  When our strength has failed
   Ere the day is half done,
     When we reach the end of our hoarded resources,
      Our Father's full giving is only begun.
 His love has no limit, His grace has no measure,
  His power has no boundary known unto men;
   For out of His infinite riches in Jesus,
    He giveth, and giveth, and giveth again."

Our part is to make that full commitment; God's promised part is to enable us to live in victory, all the while ministering to our every spiritual need. "To him who overcomes, I will give some of the hidden manna," is His promise. Ours ...is full commitment.

DON'T BE AFRAID!

"Do not be afraid, Abram."

Genesis 15:1b

Yes, God was speaking to Abraham - we know that. Some people would feel it presumptuous of us to apply it to our own hearts today - but <u>they are forgetting something</u>.

God has been speaking these same words of advice and comfort to His children through the centuries. To Israel, through Isaiah, He said,"<u>Do not fear</u>, for I am with you; do not be dismayed, for I am your God. I will strengthen you and help you. I will uphold you with My righteous right hand." Through the angel, He said to the women at the empty tomb, "<u>Do not be afraid</u> ..." And again, as those women hurried away, Jesus met them and said, "<u>Do not be afraid</u> ..." To Joshua, contemplating the conquest of the promised land, God said, "<u>Do not be afraid</u>." Again, when Joshua faced "a huge army, as numerous as the sand on the seashore," God spoke those same familiar words, "Do not be afraid ..." To Elijah, when asked to come before hostile King Ahaziah, God said, "<u>Do not be afraid</u> of him." To King Jehoshaphat, He said, "<u>Do not be afraid</u> or discouraged because of this vast army. For the battle is not yours, but God's." To Hezekiah God said, "<u>Do not be afraid</u> or discouraged ... there is a greater power with (you) than with him." Nehemiah was advised, "<u>Don't be afraid</u> of them," when he faced hostile officials in Jerusalem. To Jeremiah: "<u>Do not fear</u> them." To Ezekiel: "<u>Do not be afraid</u>." To the disciples in the storm as He came to them: "It is I. <u>Don't be afraid</u>." To Jairus: "<u>Don't be afraid</u>; just believe."

We may have no qualms about taking this word today, spoken originally to Abraham, and personalizing it as we walk along this unfamiliar and frightening pathway. In the face of troublesome treatments, plentiful pills and discouraging developments, we can stand tall and unafraid. To <u>us</u> He says firmly, "<u>Do not be afraid</u>."

AUTUMN RAINS

"If you faithfully obey the commands I am giving you ... to love the LORD your God and to serve Him with all your heart and with all your soul - then I will send rain on your land in its season, both autumn and spring rains ... "   Deuteronomy 11:13,14

We have experienced the spring rains, and love to recall the good things the Lord did for us in bygone days. He has given to us some very happy memories of joyous times together. He has blessed us with some choice Christian friends. He has provided for our every material need most graciously and bountifully. He has brought us through times of trial in triumph. He has time and again made the crooked places straight and the uneven places smooth. He has enabled for difficult tasks, and has sweetened bitter cups when we have been required to drink them. He has filled our memory bank to overflowing with happy deposits. He has provided one serendipity after another to add spice to our lives, zest to our daily experience, and heavenly dew for our dry places.

The crocus, daffodil, tulip days of our lives have been colorful, refreshing, and most welcome. We thank the Lord for them and for the abundance and regularity of those spring rains.

Yes, the spring rains came frequently and profusely. Now it is autumn for us, and we need the refreshing rains every bit as much as we did back then - perhaps more. Our leaves are getting brittle and our branches break easily. The storms of life are difficult to weather, and sometimes we shrink from this season of life. We do not have to lament the "autumn" of life, however, for we have this promise from God that our faithfulness will be rewarded with autumn rains just as He so faithfully gave the spring ones.

"... *I will send rain* on your land in its season, both *autumn and spring rains* ..."

SPIRITUAL SONGS

"Speak to one another with <u>psalms</u>, <u>hymns</u> and <u>spiritual</u> <u>songs</u>. Sing and make music in your heart to the Lord, always giving thanks to God the Father for everything, in the name of our Lord Jesus Christ."

Ephesians 5:19,20

We have been using the Psalms frequently as a source of encouragement and strength. Here Paul mentions them, but he also adds the use of hymns and of spiritual songs. From time to time we have been recalling songs. Now let's think of another one:

"Day by day, and with each passing moment,
  Strength I find to meet my trials here;
    Trusting in my Father's wise bestowment,
      I've no cause for worry or for fear.
        He whose heart is kind beyond all measure,
      Gives unto each day what He deems best -
    Lovingly, its part of pain or pleasure,
  Mingling toil with peace and rest.

Every day the Lord Himself is near me
  With a special mercy for each hour;
    All my cares He wants to bear, and cheer me,
      He whose Name is Counselor and Power.
        The protection of His child and treasure
        Is a charge that on Himself He laid;
      'As thy days, thy strength shall be in measure,'
This the pledge to me my Savior made.

Help me then, in every tribulation
  So to trust Your promises, O God,
    That I lose not faith's sweet consolation
      Offered me within Your Holy Word.
        Help me, Lord, when toil and troubles meeting
      Just to take, as from a Father's hand,
    One by one, the days, the moments fleeting,
  Till I reach the promised land."

Spiritual songs can have a profound ministry to our hearts. We gladly obey the command to make music in our hearts to the Lord. Even in the darkest hour it <u>is</u> possible to sing, at least in our hearts. Paul and Silas were singing at midnight! God invented music and it must please Him when we use it as He intended.   *

RULING PEACE

"Let the peace of Christ rule in your hearts."

Colossians 3:15

The thought of having peace reign instead of fear or pain or circumstances, is a very pleasant concept. The "peace of Christ" is a priceless commodity, and quite supernatural.

Jesus referred to it, and bequeathed it to us under very difficult circumstances when He said, "Peace I leave with you, my peace I give to you." Those words were spoken in the shadow of the cross. With the worst experiences of His life only hours away, He spoke of a "peace that passes understanding." And He was not just talking about it; He was deliberately passing it on to us!

This peace is able to keep both our hearts and our minds in amazing, unnatural tranquility in the midst of threatening circumstances. It is the same peace that enabled Paul and Silas to sing at midnight with their hands and feet locked in the stocks inside a prison.

Circumstances, no matter how bleak, cannot squelch the song of the victorious soul!

"There's a peace in my heart

That the world never gave,

A peace <u>it cannot take away</u>!

Though the trials of life

May surround like a cloud,

I've a peace that has come there <u>to stay</u>!

All the world seemed to sing

Of a Savior and King,

When <u>peace sweetly came</u> to my heart.

Troubles all fled away

And my night turned to day,

Blessed Jesus, how glorious Thou art!"

Yes, He is constantly abiding with us, and there is an element of rapture Divine in that. His "oh, so kind" whisper of the words, "I will never leave thee" minister a deep and abiding peace that is alien to this world. We must be careful to "let the peace of Christ rule in (our) hearts."

RENEW MY LIFE

"... renew my life according to Your word ... renew my life in Your righteousness ... My comfort in my suffering is this: Your promise renews my life ... He satisfies my desires with good things, so that my youth is renewed like the eagle's."   Psalm 119:37,40,50; 103:5

The word "renew" was very much a part of David's vocabulary, and a part of his experience as well. So many times God gave him a new lease on life, and He can do that for you, too.

The key to this kind of renewal seems to lie in the promises of God. David said, "My comfort in my suffering is this: Your promise renews my life."

The promises of God have been precious to us for many years. We memorized some of them, and through those years, found them to be a solid rock foundation from which to launch faith actions.

I don't think it was just the lilting melody that prompted us to sing so frequently in our childhood:

"Standing on the promises of Christ my King,
Through eternal ages let His praises ring;
Glory in the highest, I will shout and sing,
Standing on the promises of God.

Standing on the promises that cannot fail,
When the howling storms of doubt and fear assail,
By the living Word of God I shall prevail,
Standing on the promises of God."

Those wonderful promises renew our lives. We must hold fast to them now, and not let them slip from our grasp. He is capable of renewing your life as He has done so many times for others we have known (both Biblical and contemporary).

With David we must say earnestly, "Renew my life ... renew my life ... Your promise renews my life!" "My youth is renewed like the eagle's."

REST AT MIDDAY

"Tell me, you whom I love, where you graze your flock and where you <u>rest</u> your sheep <u>at midday</u>."

Song of Solomon 1:7

Midday speaks to us of that hour when the sun is the hottest, and we look for shade. In some countries a *siesta* is essential; all activity ceases and everything closes down over those unbearably hot hours. Yes, midday can be debilitating and de-energizing.

In our "midday" when the heat is on, and our activities have almost totally ground to a halt, we do well to pray this prayer of the bride in Song of Solomon: "Tell me, you whom I love, ... where you rest your sheep at midday."

He knows where there is rest to be found at midday. He is able to refresh and bless us in the midst of our trial. He calls us "the sheep of His pasture" and He loves to be our Shepherd. What a faithful Shepherd He is, leading His flock beside still waters and into the shade of protective trees.

That place of rest at midday (in the midst of our trial) is our special blessing from the Lord, our Shepherd. We must stay close to Him, so we do not miss the promised shade from the sun.

Others have passed this way before us. They have reaffirmed the truth that our Shepherd provides most graciously for His sheep, not only in the cool of the day, but also in the heat of the day. "The sun shall not smite you by day" is a promise we can claim, even during midday discomfort. Then, as surely as the passing of time brings relief from the midday sun, so shall <u>our</u> relief come. For now, while we are experiencing our midday, let's enjoy the rest He provides for His sheep, <u>even at midday</u>.

"Tell me, you whom I love, where you graze your flock and where you rest your sheep at midday."

LET CHRIST BE LORD

"... let Christ be Lord in these affairs." Romans 14:18 (L.B.)

The principle applies, even if we do lift these seven words completely out of their context. We should let Christ be Lord in <u>all</u> the affairs of life, no matter what the issue.

"King of my life, I crown Thee now; Thine shall the glory be," must be our stance through thick and thin, in sickness and in health, when we are rich or when we are poor, whether we are able to travel or are narrowly confined.

In all things, we must <u>let Christ be Lord</u>. A sublime confidence in the sovereignty of our loving Lord brings a great deal of comfort, whatever the trials of life are.

We've been through lots of things together; we've seen lots of places together. That brings to mind a gospel song. It was Andre Crouch who wrote:

"I've been to lots of places, and I've seen a lot of faces,

There've been times when I felt so all alone,

But in my lonely hours, those precious lonely hours,

    Jesus let me know that I was His own.

I thank God for the mountains,

    And I thank Him for the valleys,

I thank Him for the storms He brought me through,

    For if I'd never had a problem,

I wouldn't know that He could solve them,

    I'd never know what faith in God could do.

Through it all, through it all,

    Oh, I've learned to trust in Jesus,

     I've learned to trust in God,

Through it all, through it all,

    Oh, I've learned to depend upon His word."

So, in all these affairs of life, including the valleys as well as the mountain tops, we must "let Christ be Lord," trusting Him to weave things together in a manner that is designed for our ultimate good, even when the pattern seems strange to us, and we do not understand His workings. Our commitment must and shall be to "let Christ be Lord in these affairs."

GOD OUR MOTHER

"As a mother comforts her child, so will I comfort you."

Isaiah 66:13

It has been a long time since we were little children being rocked on our mother's lap when our ear ached. Yet we can still remember the comfort of pressing that throbbing ear against the soothing warmth of her soft bosom and whimpering there.

The pain was somewhat alleviated. The awfulness of our situation was ameliorated by her encircling arms. The intensity of the pain was mysteriously diluted by the rocking motion of the chair. We were right where we most needed to be in the midst of our pain.

Later in life we find ourselves needing the encircling arms of our Mother-God. We have been taught to pray, "Our <u>Father</u> who art in Heaven," so it is quite difficult for us to think of God as Mother. I can think of no other verse where God likens Himself to a mother. It may even be unique.

The experience spoken of here is full of comfort, as

well as of beautiful tenderness. It is the rocking chair, earache scene. God with infinite love and compassion is comforting us.

Who can tell all the tenderness of our loving God, except as she or he experiences it in moments of deep need. It is through these rocking chair episodes, when we press our throbbing body against the warmth of His beautiful promises, that we realize what a marvelous privilege it is to be a "child" of the King.

"As a <u>mother</u> comforts her child." How beautiful! How appealing! How gracious! How amazing! And how <u>very</u> special!

"As a mother comforts her child, so will I comfort you."

MY FAITHFUL SHEPHERD

"... the God who has been my Shepherd all my life to this day ..." Genesis 48:15b

Jacob had lived 147 years when he said that. That warm statement he made was backed up by more experience of trusting than we can ever hope to have. David is credited with the idea of the Lord being our Shepherd, as his twenty-third Psalm so beautifully states. But long before he penned that poetic Psalm, Jacob had called His Lord, "the God who has been my Shepherd all my life to this day."

David spelled out the implications so beautifully, including lying down in green pastures, being led by still waters, being protected by the rod and staff of the Shepherd, etc. Jacob simply lets the primary thought stand out boldly before us, without elaboration. Both men were sheep herders and knew the importance of the shepherd's actions to the well-being of the sheep. God has been our Shepherd, too - all our lives to this very day. He will continue the faithful, loving care

He has given to this point. We must never doubt that.

When we look to the future and have fears concerning what may happen to us, we are failing to remember that the Good Shepherd, <u>our</u> Good Shepherd, is not changeable, and that He even takes pride in the fact that He is unchangeable. He changes not; His compassions - they fail not. As He has been, He forever will be.

A month from now, ...six months from now, ...a year from now, or on the very last day of our lives, when it comes, we will still be able to refer to our Heavenly Father along with Jacob as "the God who has been my Shepherd all my life to <u>this</u> day."

How privileged we are to have a Gentle Shepherd to look out for our every need. We are wondrously blessed and say worshipfully, "Bless the Lord, O my soul, and all that is within me, bless His holy name!" God <u>has</u> been our Shepherd all our life, to this day!

LEARNING TO LEAN

"... your strength will equal your days ... The eternal God is your refuge, and underneath are the everlasting arms."

Deuteronomy 33:25-27

"As thy days, so shall thy strength be," was the wording we grew up on. When we first memorized this promise we were young and strong and full of vitality. Those were appealing words, even back then. They promised us something we knew we would one day be needing. That day has come!

Each new day we awaken to now is a precious gift from the Lord. It is another day to enjoy together, and in spite of the pain and medications and pills and periodic complications, He stands firmly behind His wonderful promise: "Your strength will equal your days." Yes, as our days, so shall our strength be. God's supply of strength is not going to run out before our days. "The Eternal God is our refuge and underneath are the everlasting arms."

Two songs come to mind that we have loved through

the years. The one: "What a fellowship! What a joy Divine! Leaning on the everlasting arms. What a blessedness! What a peace is mine! Leaning on the everlasting arms. Leaning, leaning, safe and secure from all alarms. Leaning, leaning, leaning on the everlasting arms." The other lyrics move us more deeply: "Learning to lean, learning to lean, I'm learning to lean on Jesus; finding more power than I ever dreamed. I'm learning to lean on Jesus."

Perhaps we are stirred more by that song because it acknowledges candidly that we have not yet fully learned how to lean on Jesus. In our spiritual frailty, we lean toward our own understanding of things instead of upon the Lord Jesus. The medical prognoses are not nearly as significant as God's promises. We must never forget that. We must lean heavily upon His everlasting arms.

"... your strength will equal your days ... The eternal God is your refuge, and underneath are the everlasting arms."

47

EMMANUEL

"... the LORD is with us. Do not be afraid ..."

Numbers 14:9d

What a comfort these words are! Our thanks must go to Caleb and Joshua who, in the face of tremendous obstacles, kept their eyes on the Lord instead of letting them linger on the giants in the land.

On many occasions in our life we have been faced with "giants" that frightened us, but I can never remember our having been overcome by any of them. God has consistently enabled us to slay those giants or to keep functioning in victory, even in the frightening presence of one of them.

Surely now, when we are faced with the tallest giant we have ever encountered, we don't have to shrink back or cower. We can remember and repeat these bold words of Caleb and Joshua: "the Lord is with us"! We do not have to be afraid.

Pain produces fear. Weakness produces fear. Even unfamiliar surroundings can produce fear, so our tendency could be to stay at home where we feel more secure. Sometimes there is no question about staying at home, for outside excursions have become out of the realm of possibility. Let's decide together once and for all that if we are able to go or if we are forced to stay, we will bask in the sunlight of Divine Sovereignty and will refuse to wallow in self pity, thinking about our limitations.

Our times are in His hand. We sang in our youth:

> "Ready to go, ready to stay,
>   Ready my place to fill;
>   Ready for service, lowly or great,
>   Ready to do His will."

That commitment has not changed. God is in control. He makes the decisions as to whether we go or stay. We will please Him by our submissiveness, never fearing, for the LORD is with us!

COVERED!

"I have ... covered you with the shadow of my hand ..."

Isaiah 51:16

Shadows are sometimes associated with troubles: "the valley of the shadow of death," for example. But there is also a very positive connotation to the word "shadow" that is deeply appreciated by those who live where shelter from the sun's devastation is an important factor in their lives. To them a shadow is most welcome. The shade of a tree is often sought by people parking their cars. The shadow an awning casts is considered well worth the price of that addition to their homes.

So, the shadow of God's hand becomes a very precious and appreciated protection from the heat of our days. It is more personal than the gourd-plant that God grew to shield Jonah, for it is His own hand, positioned in protection over us that is providing the welcome relief.   *

"Faint from the heat and the length of the road,
 I was oppressed by a wearisome load;
  One came so tenderly saying to me:
   'Give me thy load, it's too heavy for thee.'
  Jesus Himself, <u>Jesus Himself</u>!

What though the valleys be many and deep,
 What if the pathway be stony or steep;
  Mountain or moorland or valley of death:
   'I will be with thee,' my Comforter saith.
  Jesus Himself, <u>Jesus Himself</u>!"

The promise of being covered with the shadow of
God's own hand is a very beautiful and comforting
one, filled with tenderness and love.

"I have ... covered you with the shadow of my hand ..."

BY THE POWER OF JESUS

"I live by the power of the living Father who sent Me, and in the same way those who partake of Me shall live because of Me!"   John 6:57 (L.B.)

Here is a profound truth that we cannot fully grasp without the enabling of the Holy Spirit. All through the life of the Lord Jesus He made it abundantly clear that He was drawing upon Divine strength, wisdom, and enabling every moment.

He lived as a human being, though He was God come in the flesh. He demonstrated to us with perfection the life lived in the power of Another. He chose to model for us the way a human could be Divinely enabled, though that was not essential.

We wish we could understand more perfectly what it means to "partake" of Him. Those who heard Him speak didn't understand it. In fact, when He elaborated upon the importance of "eating" His flesh and "drinking" His blood, they said, "This is a difficult truth; who can understand it?" He was not speaking of partaking of the communion elements, but of something much deeper and mystically significant. They couldn't comprehend that.

Oh, that the Lord would this day teach us more about drawing upon <u>His</u> strength, <u>His</u> life, and <u>His</u> limitless vitality. There are secrets to be learned that we are eager to know. We want to experience the resurrection power of the Lord Jesus flowing through these mortal bodies, just as He experienced that from His Father on Easter Day when He was raised from the dead.

Surely disease cannot survive the presence of the Holy Spirit in His fullness. Our prayer is for a new infilling of His Holy Spirit not only because of the wondrous joy of fullness, but also because of the expulsive power of such Divine Life. It can surely expel all that is foreign and destructive, and not of God. *"I live by the power of the living Father who sent Me, and in the same way <u>those who partake of Me shall live because of Me</u>!"*

A FIRM FOUNDATION

"God's solid foundation stands firm, sealed with this inscription: 'The Lord knows those who are His.'"

II Timothy 2:19a

At a time in your life when there are so many changes, ...when your strength has diminished, ...when pain has entered the picture, ...when the prognosis of the doctor gives us little hope, it is a great encouragement to remind our hearts that "God's foundation stands firm" and that He "knows those who are His."

You and I are His. We belong to Him, and on this firm foundation that is ours there is an inscription reaffirming our relationship to Him. It is a beautiful picture. Observe the firm, almost musical, foundation to these beautiful lyrics, "God's solid foundation stands firm, sealed with this inscription: 'The Lord knows those who are His.'"

On Christ, the Solid Rock we stand. What a comfort when we are so deeply aware that all other ground is sinking sand! "His oath, His covenant, His blood, support me in the overwhelming flood. When all around my soul gives way, He then is all my hope and stay." Yes, we have a strong foundation, and we can rejoice in that.

"How firm a foundation, you saints of the Lord, is laid for your faith in His excellent word!" the hymn writer penned. But it was God Himself who penned the words of this text. Let's hear them a third time: "God's solid foundation stands firm, sealed with this inscription: 'The Lord knows those who are His.'"

That's a reminder that He knows all about us. He knows every detail of what we are going through. He knows every cell in your body. He knows what the best healing procedures are for you, even when our doctors are stumped, or admittedly limited. He is our Great Physician, and we can revel in the fact that He is a Doctor who still makes house calls! You are His, and He knows you very well. Take heart in His own reaffirmation: *

GOD LOVES TO BE LIKE HE IS

"I am the Lord of justice and of righteousness whose love is steadfast; and I love to be this way."

Jeremiah 9:24b (L.B.)

Our understanding of who God is and what He is like includes all of the above-mentioned: justice, righteousness, and love. We know that. Do we also know that God enjoys being like that? "I love to be this way," are His intriguing words!

God loves to love. He loves to see justice triumph. He loves to promote righteousness, and He enjoys seeing it in His people. But the one of these three that is the most personal and beautiful is His love for loving.

He has loved us with an eternal love. He has shed that love abroad in our hearts. In His love He has showered us with good things, but always with the full knowledge of what is best for us and never indulging us like some parents do their children. He knows what is detrimental to us, and in His love, He even withholds some things, so that we will not be spoiled or destroyed by them.

We love to have Him as He is, and have told Him so, many times. But perhaps this is the first time that we have noticed the statement that God <u>enjoys</u> being loving as He is.

The more closely we walk with God, the more we too will be able to be happy with who we are, and how we are. We should have personal characteristics about which we too can say that we love to be that way. When we spontaneously reach out to the hurting, we should be able to say that we love to be that way. When we pray with a burdened heart for our missionary friends, we should love to be that way. It is a blessing to remember that God loves to love, He loves to give, <u>and He loves to be that way</u>!

"I am the Lord of justice and of righteousness whose love is steadfast; and I love to be this way."

GOD MADE BOTH

"When times are good, be happy; but when times are bad, consider: <u>God has made the one as well as the other.</u>"

Ecclesiastes 7:14

We praise God for the good times - easily, gladly, joyfully. We do not thank Him for the bad times. That's an unnatural thing to do. In fact, it goes against our grain. Yet here we are reminded that "God has made the one as well as the other."

Bad times are <u>not</u> enjoyable. Bitter usually has no sweetness about it. Yet things can be bittersweet. Sour is always sour - but is it <u>always</u>? In a good Chinese restaurant some of the most delectable dishes are listed on the menu as "sweet 'n sour."

These (years) that we have been battling (cancer) have often been characterized by bitter experiences like pain, hospitals, treatments, weakness, discouragement, etc. But we readily acknowledge that there has been a bittersweet aspect to this difficult period in our lives. The sweet memories we have of God-given deliverances would not be ours if we had not encountered adversities, pain, and even desperately difficult times. God knew that, and in His loving wisdom He permitted our bad times. We can somewhat readily acknowledge that God permitted the difficulty, but this verse goes beyond that and reminds us that He made the bad times. That's hard for us to swallow! Notice, though, that we are told to be happy when times are good, but we are not asked to be happy when times are bad. We are only asked to consider that "God has made the one as well as the other."

We must ask ourselves the question, "Shall we accept good from God, and not trouble?" (Job 2:10) No, by His grace we will accept both. On either kind of day we will say, "This is the day the Lord has made; let us rejoice and be glad in it." (Psalm 118:24)

"When times are good, be happy; but when times are bad, consider: God has made the one as well as the other."

HE CARES FOR YOU

"Do not fear ... do not be frightened. But in your hearts set apart Christ as Lord. ... do not be surprised at the painful trial you are suffering, as though something strange were happening to you. But rejoice that you participate in the sufferings of Christ, so that you may be overjoyed when His glory is revealed. ... Cast all your anxiety on Him because He cares for you."

I Peter 3,4,5 (excerpts)

It is very normal for us to be fearful of the twists and turns of this dark valley through which we are passing. We don't know exactly what developments lie ahead of us before He completely delivers us from this "painful trial." Even doctors cannot predict with any degree of certainty what lies in store for us - thankfully. "If we could see, if we could know, we often say; but God, in love, a veil doth throw across our way; We cannot see what lies before, and so we cling to Him the more. He leads us till this life is o'er, (we'll just) trust and obey."

"<u>Do not fear</u>," "<u>Do not be frightened</u>," "<u>Do not be surprised</u>." Fears come easily and naturally to us. We must exchange that for hope and peace coming easily and naturally. The Lord Jesus can do that for us. Each new day can be faced confidently as we walk hand in hand with Jesus through this vale of tears. We can <u>and will</u> cast our anxiety on Him, knowing that He cares for us in the midst of this severe trial every bit as much as He did in the days when we traveled and served and ministered together outside the walls of this little home.

"All our anxiety, all our care,
(We'll) bring to the mercy seat and leave it there.
There's never a burden that He cannot bear.
There was never a friend like Jesus!"

We must not forget this admonition: "Do not fear - do not be frightened"! *

JOY STRENGTH!

"... the joy of the LORD is your strength."

Nehemiah 8:10c

This verse ties in with the one that tells us that a merry heart is good medicine. Here we are told that joy and strength are in some special way linked, as well.

Earth's joys are so transient, but the joy of the Lord is quite the opposite. There is nothing that can take it from us when we tenaciously hold on to it.

Our sustenance in this battle has not come through medications and treatments, but rather through a spiritual provision that goes far beyond what a person outside of Jesus Christ has.

"We've a peace in our hearts that the world never gave
- a peace it cannot take away.

Though the trials of life may surround like a cloud,
we've a peace that has come there to stay!"

Hopefully tonight will be a good night and tomorrow another good day, but the foundation of our joy is not to be found in good nights and days; it is solidly laid in our relationship to the Lord Jesus, and that never changes. "Change and decay in all around I see; Oh, Thou who changest not, abide with me."

Because He is the Changeless One, we do not have to be significantly affected by the multitude of changes we see everywhere. Our world is changing on fast forward (perhaps "fast-backward" would be a more appropriate word). Our bodies are changing, too. The prospect of the future is not terribly exciting for either of us! We don't have our heads in the sand; we recognize that our physical strength is diminishing, but that has very little to do with the strength the joy of the Lord provides. That strength is special, even phenomenal. It is there for us and for anyone who will drink deeply of the joy of the Lord.

"The joy of the Lord is (our) strength!"

WORRY ABOUT LIFE!

"... do not worry about your life ... consider the ravens: ... God ... (takes care of them). ... how much more valuable you are than birds! Who of you by worrying can add a single hour to his life? Since you cannot do this very little thing, why do you worry about the rest?"

Luke 12:22-26

Worrying about life is almost a reflexive, intuitive act. We have to admit, however, that we are incapable of adding a single hour to our life and that our times are in God's hands. So, it makes little sense for us to worry about our life, yet we seem to persist in this admittedly futile mental exercise.

May God enable us to commit ourselves to Him so thoroughly that we are set free from this fruitless worry. May His interest in birds, and His care for them reassure us that we, who are so much more valuable than birds, will be wonderfully cared for, too. When we review our lives thoughtfully, we can only marvel over the watchful care our Heavenly Father has given us. He has protected us so many times. He has provided for us when we didn't know where provision was coming from. He has restored our health more than once. He has guided our footsteps so definitely and decisively, even when they took us where others looked askance at our judgment (or seeming lack of it). He has moved upon people to help us generously when we have had a need. He has given us comfortable, enjoyable homes in which to live. He has provided a host of good friends who stick by us consistently in times of trouble. He has blessed our various ministries for Him. Most recently, He has been walking with us and supporting us faithfully through this dark valley of the shadow of death. Why should we _ever_ worry about our lives? God has clearly and forcefully admonished us, "Do not worry about your life."

TRUE LIFE

"... take hold of the life that is truly life."

I Timothy 6:19b

The implication is that there is a higher quality of life than we have been experiencing in our brief earthly existence. We know that's true and for years have been giving mental assent. Now we are faced with a life-threatening condition that forces us to place everything solidly in eternal perspective.

The "life that is truly life" became our wonderful gift from God the moment we placed our faith in the Lord Jesus, so many years ago. It has meant ever so much to us through the years of our earth-bound journey to know that we possessed eternal life that could never be taken from us. Now this verse has even more significance to us, when physical life is being threatened and our happy years of living and serving God together seem to be winding down.

It is very human for us to cling to the relationship we have enjoyed, and to pray earnestly for the preservation of life. We will not give up on praying for the miracle that can so easily be granted by our gracious, all-powerful Lord. But while we wait we must be careful to cling tenaciously to the "<u>life that is truly life</u>."

How different that life is! It is unaffected by time, for eternity is the air it breathes. It is never touched by illness, for illness is a result of the fall and is limited to earth's confines, having no place in Heaven. No pain is allowed past those gates, and the bodies we shall enjoy there are totally immune to anything destructive.

Ah, Life with a capital "L" not only awaits us, but also is in prototype ours <u>right</u> <u>now</u> to enjoy. We will deliberately take hold of the "life that is truly life," and rejoice in it.

THE PSALMS

"*The righteous cry out and the Lord hears them; He delivers them from all their troubles. The Lord is close to the brokenhearted and saves those who are crushed in spirit. A righteous person may have many troubles, but the Lord delivers him from them all. Trust in the Lord and do good. Delight yourself in the Lord and He will give you the desires of your heart. Commit your way to the Lord; trust in Him. God is our refuge and strength, an ever present help in trouble. Therefore we will not fear. Great is the Lord and most worthy of praise. Be still and know that I am God. Why should I fear when evil days come? This God is our God forever and ever; I trust in God's unfailing love, forever and ever. I will praise Him for what He has done. In His name I will hope, for His name is good. I will cast my cares on the Lord and He will sustain me. He will never let the righteous fall. As for me, I will trust in Him. When I am afraid, I will trust in Him, in God, whose word I praise. In God, I trust; I will not be afraid. He has delivered my soul from death and my feet from stumbling. Great is Your love, reaching to the heavens; Your faithfulness reaches to the skies. I will sing of Your strength, in the morning I will sing of Your love; You are my fortress, my refuge in times of trouble. O my Strength, I will sing praise to You; You, O God, are my fortress, my loving God. Praise be to the Lord, to God our Savior, who daily bears our burdens. Our God is a God who saves, from the Sovereign Lord comes escape from death. Show us Your strength, O God, as You have done before. Though You have made me see troubles, many and bitter, You will restore my life again. I will praise You for Your faithfulness, O my God; I will sing praise to You. As for me, it is good to be near God."*

TAKE IT BY THE TAIL!

"... the LORD said to him, 'What is that in your hand?'
'A staff,' he replied ... The LORD said, 'Throw it on the
ground.' Moses threw it on the ground and it became a
snake, and <u>he ran from it</u>. The LORD said to him,
'<u>Reach out your hand and take it by the tail</u>.' So <u>Moses</u>
reached out and <u>took hold of the snake and it turned</u>
back <u>into a staff</u> in his hand." ·   Exodus 4:2-4

It is good to realize that turning over to God what we
have in our hand is not only the right thing to do, but
also it is a very valuable action. Much more is being
taught here than that, however.

God was teaching Moses that what he had in his hand
was the power to turn a snake into a staff! That's far
more significant than the turning of the staff into a
snake. For that to happen, all he had to do was to
throw it down, but...

To change a snake into a staff (a harmful thing into a
helpful thing) takes special Divine power, <u>coupled</u>
<u>with</u> personal courage. It doesn't take any courage to

70

throw a stick away, but it surely does to pick up a snake - especially a poisonous one!

We know the snake was poisonous because Moses ran from it. He was a man who almost certainly knew his reptiles. You don't take care of sheep for forty years in a wilderness without knowing which snakes are poisonous. No, Moses would not have fled from a non-poisonous snake.

We, too, have the privilege of taking by the tail the terrifying things in life and watching them turn into helpful triumphs by God's power. So, it makes a great deal of difference whether what we have in our hand is an ordinary or a miracle staff. What was in Moses' hand looked the same, but was very different after that!

"The LORD said to him, 'Reach out your hand and take it by the tail.' So Moses reached out and took hold of the snake and it turned back into a staff in his hand."

SPIRITUAL BLESSINGS!

"Praise be to the God and Father of our Lord Jesus Christ, who has blessed us ... with every <u>spiritual blessing</u>."   Ephesians 1:3

Our hearts spontaneously leap up in praise when we meditate upon the multitude of spiritual blessings with which God has enriched us. We are very well-to-do in the things of the Spirit.

The value of our eternal salvation is inestimable. The beauty of fellowship with God, which has been restored to us, can only be fully experienced, not adequately described. The awesome privilege of being a joint-heir with Jesus Christ staggers our mind. The priceless gift of eternal life defies the ability of the finite mind to comprehend (how can the finite comprehend the infinite?).

We praise the Lord, who has so richly blessed us. His wisdom and knowledge are boundless, and He has generously given some to us, for "Christ Jesus ... has become for us wisdom from God." His power is limitless and He has placed that power at our disposal through fabulous prayer promises such as, "I will do anything you ask in my name, so that the Son may bring glory to the Father. You may ask me for <u>anything</u> in my name, and I will do it." (John 14:13,14) His love is incomparable, and He has lavishly showered it upon us, loving us with an everlasting love. His sovereignty coupled with His beneficent nature guarantees to us that everything shall continue to work together for our good - eternally!

Yes, He has blessed us with all spiritual blessings, and even when we have a deficiency in the area of physical blessings, we can remind ourselves that this physical problem is only temporary. We have a brand new body coming that cannot be touched by earth's diseases and will not deteriorate with age. How rich we are - how <u>very</u> rich we are!

"Praise be to the God and Father of our Lord Jesus Christ, who has blessed us ... with every spiritual blessing."

REFUGE AND STRENGTH

"God is our <u>refuge and strength</u>, an ever present help in trouble. Therefore we will not fear."

Psalm 46:1,2a

Cards and notes come from friends regularly these days. It is an encouragement to know that we are remembered and that there are so many friends who are praying. We receive a definite renewal of our strength as they pray. We are aware of that.

Many cards include a Scripture verse or reference. One of the most popular ones is this: "God is our refuge and strength, an ever present help in trouble." We know the verse well, but right now we need those reminders. God is no ordinary source of refuge and strength. He is all-powerful and His refuge is perfect.

"Under His wings I am safely abiding;
   Though the night deepens and tempests are wild,
   Still I can trust Him, I know He will keep me;
   He has redeemed me, and I am His child.

74

Under His wings, what a refuge in sorrow!
How the heart yearningly turns to His rest!
Often when earth has no balm for my healing,
There I find comfort and there I am blest.
Under His wings my soul shall abide,
Safely abide forever."

Yes. God is indeed our refuge and our strength! But the Psalmist went on to say, "<u>Therefore we will not fear</u>." When the medical prognosis is bleak it becomes easier to fear than it is to trust. That is only because we are listening to the <u>prognosis</u> rather than to God's <u>promise</u>. When our enemy attempts to come in like a flood, we must learn to flee to our Refuge and unlimited Source of Strength and not be disheartened. "We <u>will not</u> fear"! We refuse to fear. We <u>will</u> rest! And we <u>will</u> trust!

"God is our refuge and strength, an ever present help in trouble. Therefore we will not fear."

HE MADE ALL THINGS

"Through Him all things were made; without Him nothing was made that has been made."   John 1:3

<u>We must remember this</u> when we look at the exquisite intricacies of flower after flower.   Infinite variety, superb form, subtle hues and unbelievable detail are all in evidence upon close examination of even the simplest of flowers, let alone the fuschia or the passion flower or the triple hibiscus. He designed it all. He chose its fragrance. He sculpted its original petals.   *
<u>We must remember this</u> when we gaze with awe upon the majesty of the mountains, with ranges that differ in character and beauty. The treeless Grand Tetons are as beautiful in their own way as the heavily treed Black Hills of South Dakota. The snow capped Sierra Nevada <u>range</u> of mountains is impressive, but so are the <u>individual</u> volcanic peaks of the West Coast like Mount Shasta, Mount Baker, and Mount Ranier. Each in its own way inspires worship from deep within the sensitive soul.   *

<u>We must remember this</u> when we stand at the edge of the ocean and marvel at the power of its pounding waves. We look out over the expanse before our eyes and cannot fully imagine its vastness. We stare at the rolling, crashing, rebounding waves and realize with amazement that they persist hour after hour, day after day, month after month, *ad infinitum.*   *

<u>We must remember this</u> when we look at the bodies God has given us with detail and complexity that evoke a worshipful wonder from even the most scientific. Our completely automatic dual cameras, our two-thousand stringed dual pianos miniaturized to fit inside our ears, our delicately balanced chemical factory; He made them all - <u>He made them all</u>! And remember, He knows how to repair what He has made.

"Through Him all things were made; without Him nothing was made that has been made."

ONE DAY AT A TIME

"God will take care of your tomorrow ... <u>Live</u>
<u>one day at a time</u>." Matthew 6:34 (L.B.)

The expression, "Live one day at a time," has become
such common advice that we easily forget it is not just
a trite 20th century piece of advice. God spoke those
words to us through Matthew, long ago.

We <u>have</u> been living one day at a time and finding
grace for each new day. God's own provision of
"hidden manna" has been all we have needed to
sustain us, even on the darkest of our days. Well-
known promises have become foundational truths that
let us stand tall and strong even in difficult times. "As
your days, so shall your strength be," has been newly
proven every 24 hours!

"One day at a time." That's how we're handling it,
but while we apply the "one day at a time" principle
to living, let's never forget the other half of the verse;
"God will take care of your tomorrow."

All our tomorrows are in His hand. He knows right

now what each will be like and exactly what we will need. All our todays are in His hand, too! It seems as if our days are flying past us in spite of relative inactivity. Time is a strange thing; sometimes it flies and sometimes it drags, in spite of a scientific constancy that is precise. Our times are in His hands ...our todays, ...our tomorrows - that is our comfort. So, we live <u>one</u> <u>day</u> <u>at</u> <u>a</u> <u>time</u>, committing tomorrow to our loving Heavenly Father, remembering that He will take care of all of our times as we simply commit them to Him, even our every moment!

"Moment by moment I'm kept in His love;
Moment by moment I've life from above;
Looking to Jesus 'till glory doth shine;
Moment by moment, O Lord, I am thine."

Let's remember with joy that "God will take care of (our) tomorrow" and just "live one day at a time."

NOT OVERWHELMED

"... this is what the LORD says - He who created you ... He who formed you ... 'Fear not for I have redeemed you; I have called you by name; you are mine. When you pass through the waters, I will be with you; and when you pass through the rivers, they will not sweep over you. When you walk through the fire, you will not be burned ... for I am the LORD your God, the Holy One of Israel, your Savior ... Do not be afraid, for I am with you.'"

Isaiah 43:1-5

We were never promised exemption from trial. "When you pass through the waters..." and "When you walk through the fire..." are implying that we most certainly will have trials. The comforting promise is that they will not overwhelm us. Our loving Lord is in control, even on the darkest of days; even when the fires are the hottest; even when the rivers are the deepest. "I am the Lord your God," He reminds us. Our part is to remind our own hearts of this regularly, so that the enemy of our souls cannot gain a victory in our minds. There is no river that is going to drown us. There is no fire that is going to burn us. We belong to the Sovereign of the universe. He is caring for our every need and watching over us lovingly and carefully as we pass through this severe difficulty.

As we think back over the days of this trial, we have to acknowledge that the Lord <u>has</u> helped us wonderfully. He has brought one encouragement after another: cards, phone calls, food, etc. These special blessings that have come so steadily are all parts of the loving watchcare of our ever present Lord. We shall cross this river in triumph together. We shall not even have the smell of smoke upon us when we come out of this fire, by the grace and with the help of our God.

"When you pass through the waters, I will be with you; and when you pass through the rivers, they will not sweep over you. When you walk through the fire, you will not be burned ... for I am the LORD your God ..."

NO ENTRANCE!

"... the LORD ... <u>will not permit</u> the destroyer to enter your houses and strike you down."   Exodus 12:23

It was the blood on the top and sides of the doorframe that protected the children of Israel. That blood was a symbol of their obedience, as well as of their faith in the promises of God.

By faith in His strong promises and Person, <u>we</u> have the blood on the doorposts of <u>our</u> hearts and we come under the wondrous protection of the blood of Christ. Our position is both safe and <u>very</u> secure.

"Precious, precious blood of Jesus, shed on Calvary. Shed for lost ones; shed for sinners; shed for <u>me</u>," is the joyous response of our hearts. We can rejoice over the fact that no destroyer can get past that protection. Our times are in His hands, and the enemy of our souls has no say about the length of our lives. God controls that.

"The LORD <u>will not permit</u> the destroyer to strike you down." There is a comforting definiteness about those words. They remind us that our God is in absolute, firm and final control. We are immortal until our life's work is done, come what may. There is not one thing our enemy can do about that. We must rest secure in that knowledge.

There is tremendous power in the blood of Christ that makes Satan back away. He has never been able to touch the one under its protection without special permission from the Lord Himself, and even in that instance, only temporarily and with a specific purpose in God's mind. Our God is all powerful, and "He's got the whole world in His hand ... He's got you and me in His hand." He will not permit the destroyer to enter our house and strike us down.

MY FRAGRANCE

"While the king was at his table, my perfume spread its fragrance ... Awake, north wind, and come, south wind! Blow on my garden, that its fragrance may spread abroad."   Song of Solomon 1:12; 4:16

"My perfume" and "my fragrance" are both spoken of here. It is easy to forget that there is a fragrance that exudes from the life that is totally committed to Christ. We have enjoyed that sweet perfume in others, but quite appropriately have not recognized it in ourselves.

The first of these two verses indicates that <u>fellowship releases fragrance</u>, for it is while the King sits at His table with me that my fragrance spreads. The second one implies that <u>trouble and triumph release fragrance</u>, for it is the north wind <u>and</u> the south wind that spread it abroad.

The south winds have always been most welcome, but these north winds we find difficult to take. We have never been able to pray the prayer, "Awake, north

wind, and come, south wind, blow on my garden."
But we do not have to pray that prayer to experience
the dual winds of adversity and prosperity - they come
uninvited! It is the north winds that are blowing on
our garden right now. Shall we lament them, or shall
we invite them to cause the fragrance of our garden to
be spread abroad?

Some fragrances are released by warm winds that cause
the blossom to open and the fragrance to emanate.
Some fragrances are released when the harsh, cold
north winds bruise and crush, and in the process,
fragrance is released. The mint that grows by the side
of our house is extra fragrant when I take a leaf
between thumb and forefinger and crush it, or at least
bruise it. As the north winds bruise and attempt to
crush us, may it please God to let a fragrance be
released from within us.

"... Awake, north wind, and come, south wind! Blow on
my garden, that its fragrance may spread abroad."

LOVE-STRENGTH COMBO

"In Your unfailing love You will lead the people You have redeemed. In Your strength You will guide them to Your holy dwelling."   Exodus 15:13

This verse is worthy of memorization, yet it is not one of the standard ones the Lord's people tend to zero in on.

God's guidance is spoken of twice here. First it is coupled with unfailing love, and then it is linked with His great strength. What a combination!

God's strength is activated on our behalf by His unfailing love. That's a win/win situation! There is no losing, <u>ever</u>, when our all-powerful God, knowing every little detail of our existence by virtue of His omniscience, decides to intervene in our lives because of His unfailing, unlimited love.

A sincere "Hallelujah!" should well up in our hearts as we think about that. God paid a great price for us, and He is not all that different from us in wanting to preserve that for which He has paid a great price. We don't think of ourselves as "pearls of great price," yet He implies that we are, for we are being changed into Christ's likeness.

Basking in the warmth of another's love is a beautiful thing. We have loved each other deeply, sincerely, and consistently. Yet our love pales in significance when compared with the love with which <u>He</u> has loved us!

"O, <u>perfect</u> love, all human loves transcending!
   Lowly we kneel in prayer before Thy throne,
That (ours, too) may be the love which knows
      no ending,
   Whom Thou forevermore (hast) joined in one."

God's love combined with His unlimited strength exercised on our behalf is a very beautiful and a very comforting privilege.

"In Your unfailing love You will lead the people You have redeemed. In Your strength You will guide them to Your holy dwelling."

LOOKING UNTO JESUS

"Let us <u>fix our eyes on Jesus</u>, the author and perfecter of our faith ... Consider Him who endured ... so that you will not grow weary and lose heart."   Hebrews 12:2,3

It is quite human to <u>grow weary</u> and to <u>lose heart</u> after waiting and waiting for the miracle we have been praying for. It helps to remember how much <u>He</u> endured, and how faithful <u>He</u> was through it all.

His three and one half ministering years here on earth must have been very painful for Him, quite apart from the awful physical pain of the beating and the cross. The pain of facing unbelief, criticism, misunderstanding, and false accusation was no small trial in itself. Yet He plodded on faithfully, knowing fully where His path was leading and that worse suffering was still ahead of Him.

This suffering Savior is the One who authors and perfects faith in us! We must (1) let sorrow do her work, (2) allow suffering to teach us to lean heavily upon Him, (3) perfect our submission to His finely honed, beautiful plan, and (4) glean from these dark clouds every silver lining we can find.

The words in this text, "Let us fix our eyes on Jesus" must have been the inspiration for Helen Lemmel when she wrote:

"O, soul, are you weary and troubled?
    No light in the darkness you see?
  There's light for a look at the Savior,
    And life more abundant and free!
  Turn your eyes upon Jesus,
    Look full in His wonderful face;
  And the things of earth will grow strangely dim
    In the light of His glory and grace."

"Let us fix our eyes on Jesus, the author and perfecter of our faith ... Consider Him who endured ... so that you will not grow weary and lose heart."

INCREDIBLE POWER!

"I pray that you will begin to understand how incredibly great His power is to help those who believe Him."

Ephesians 1:19 (L.B.)

His "incredibly great power." That's what Paul calls it. It is a power <u>so</u> great that it is beyond our comprehension.

Once in awhile we catch a glimpse of it, as when God does something special that is above and beyond what man can take credit for. Then our hearts eagerly respond, "Yes, His power <u>is</u> incredibly great. There is nothing too hard for the Lord!" The truth is that the scope of His power extends outward forever, like the universe itself. Man has been grappling with the concept of an ever-expanding universe for years. It's a theory too big for his little mind.

We live in an incredibly great universe, the creation of our incredibly great God by use of His incredibly great power. But the marvel of <u>this</u> text is that God says His power is exercised on <u>our</u> behalf! This verse could so logically have stopped after saying, "I pray that you will begin to understand how incredibly great His power is." But it does <u>not</u> stop there; it goes on to read, "<u>to help those who believe Him</u>."

That incredible power is there for me, it is there for you! We must let nothing rob us of that truth. Not pain, nor weakness, nor fear, nor life's storms. God is God. His incredibly great power has never been diminished even minutely by exercising it. Nor has it been adversely affected one iota by man's attempts to limit and define Him. We will trust Him to use that power on our behalf in each new day in whatever ways He chooses. We will face tomorrow expecting Him to exhibit His incredibly great power, perhaps even in ways that will greatly please <u>us</u>, as well as to greatly glorify <u>Him</u>.

"I pray that you will begin to understand how incredibly great His power is to help those who believe Him."

IN ALL CIRCUMSTANCES

"... give thanks <u>in all circumstances</u>, for this is God's will for you in Christ Jesus."   I Thessalonians 5:18

To give thanks <u>for</u> all circumstances would be virtually impossible, but to give thanks <u>in</u> all circumstances is not. We can, in every circumstance of life, no matter how dark or difficult or painful, find reasons for giving thanks.

We have so very many of them. Among the best reasons for thanksgiving are the spiritual gifts God has given. Those can <u>never</u> be taken from us under <u>any</u> circumstance. Our salvation is a very precious gift from our loving Savior. The price He paid for that included pain of a kind we will never suffer. No one can ever fully comprehend the depth of that pain, for there is none righteous, no not one. Only a totally righteous person could fully grasp how painful it was for Him to be made sin for us.

Another cause for thankfulness, even in our current circumstance, is the relationship we enjoy with one another. It is beautiful, and it is what God designed it to be: deep, meaningful and sustaining. We have each other. That is a priceless gift from God, and we can both enjoy the security that gift provides.

There are comforts that are ours that also have special meaning in the way of a comfortable home, a host of very special friends, access to caring doctors, and ever so many other joys. It is not difficult to find <u>many</u> reasons for giving thanks.

We must remember that praise is often a prelude to victory. We will offer together the sacrifice of praise and it will be pleasing to God. Even in these circumstances, we can know the victory of praise-filled hearts. This is God's will for us, we are told, and in Christ Jesus we can do it!

"... give thanks in all circumstances, for this is God's will for you in Christ Jesus."

HOPING CONTRARY

"Standing before God, Abraham believed God makes the dead live and calls into being that which doesn't exist. Hoping contrary to what he could expect, he had the faith to become the father of many nations, as he had been told ... He didn't get weak in faith, although he realized that, being about a hundred years old, he couldn't have children any more, and Sarah couldn't have any either. There was no unbelief to make him doubt what God promised ... He was fully convinced that God could do what He promised." Romans 4:17-21 (Beck)

Oh for the faith of Abraham, who took God at His word and didn't worry about how absurd the promise appeared to others, or how impossible it was scientifically, or how unreasonable it was to hope for a child at their age! The promise ran contrary to all man knows about the human body, as well as to the history of mankind. There was no precedent for this kind of miracle, with the single exception of the making of a human body out of a human rib.

94

No, Abraham didn't have anything to encourage him to believe except a promise from God, but He saw any promise from his promise-keeping God as more than enough of a foundation for belief. He hoped "<u>contrary to what he could expect</u>."

Let's keep doing that together. We must never give up hoping; it would be foolish to do that when we have had such wonderful promises given to us in the Word of the Lord. We will keep claiming them, even in the face of the symptoms "bad days" bring with them. The doctors call that stance "denial", but we don't see it that way. We see it as following in the footsteps of a man whose ridiculous faith greatly pleased the Lord - <u>so</u> greatly, in fact, that God responded to his faith and gave him what He had promised him. May the Lord give us hope <u>contrary to what we can expect</u> if we listen only to our doctors. He can do that!   *

HE REACHED DOWN

"He reached down from on high and took hold of me; He drew me out of deep waters."　　Psalm 18:16

When the artist painted a giant hand reaching down out of a stormy sky toward an angry sea in which a person was sinking, he so graphically depicted the promise in this verse.

More dramatic yet is the literal fulfillment of this promise when we find ourselves troubled by deep waters (as we do now) and *we* experience the lifting up by means of that giant hand of God.

God has indeed helped us. He has given grace for each day. He has renewed strength from time to time. He has brought one serendipity after another into our lives, such as flowers that came from unexpected sources, and the assurances of regular prayer support from people we didn't know cared that much. He has helped us not to cast away our confidence, even when faced with pain and weakness.

Deep waters never did frighten Him, like they do us.

He walked <u>on</u> the troubled waters, putting them <u>beneath</u> His feet. We worry about their going <u>over</u> our heads! It is well for us to slip our hand into His and enjoy the feeling of having all these troubles beneath <u>our</u> feet as well. They may not be gone, but whether they are <u>beneath our feet</u> or <u>over our heads</u>, makes a world of difference.

"He reached down." What a beautiful condescension! It amazes us to think that His mighty hand reaches down to this small house on our little street, right into this room where His children need Him. There He lifts us up, encourages us, and repeats to us His loving promises.

"He reached down from on high and took hold of me; He drew me out of deep waters."

THE PRAYERS OF MANY

"We were under great pressure, far beyond our ability to endure, so that we despaired even of life. Indeed, in our hearts we felt the sentence of death. But this happened that we might not rely on ourselves, but on God, who raises the dead. <u>He has delivered us</u> from a deadly peril, and <u>He will deliver us</u>. On Him we have set our hope that <u>He will continue to deliver us</u>, as you help us by your prayers. Then many will give thanks on our behalf for the gracious favor granted us in answer to <u>the prayers of many</u>."   II Corinthians 1:8b-11

Every day we are reminded by way of phone calls and cards of the faithful prayers of <u>so</u> many. We have been amazed over the number of people who have said, "We pray for you every day"! Sometimes they have been people whom we would not have expected to be that concerned or faithful. They don't know us that well. We feel strongly that it is God who has laid us on their hearts.

Shouldn't that fill us with an expectation of good

things? God has heard these many prayers. He has already answered in part by giving grace for these trials, and strength to face each new day. He who has begun this good work will surely bring it to a victorious completion, "in answer to the prayers of many."

"This happened that we might not rely upon ourselves but on God," Paul said. We must discipline ourselves to rely totally upon God in the midst of this severe trial. He has proven Himself faithful through all the years of our earthly pilgrimage and He will surely continue to do that now, when we most need Him.

"In answer to the prayers of many..." That's not a familiar phrase. Let's be encouraged by it as we, too, count upon the prayers of many and the faithfulness of our prayer-answering God to hear each one and to respond so lovingly.

"Then many will give thanks on our behalf for the gracious favor granted us in answer to the prayers of many."

HEAVEN'S DEW

"May God give you of <u>heaven's dew</u> and of <u>earth's</u> <u>richness</u> ... "   Genesis 27:28

We have enjoyed earth's richness. Though we have not been wealthy like some of our friends, we have had more than enough. We do not subscribe to the currently popular prosperity theology, but we do remember that from those earliest days when we had so very little, God faithfully provided for us every time we had a need. That has been true right to the present when we are adequately cared for in every area. God has blessed us with the richness of the earth.

Heaven's dew is much more significant to us now. The lustre of earth's richness is fading. Tarnish is beginning to appear more quickly than we can remove it, and we even get tired of the polishing. So we turn our eyes increasingly toward heaven's refreshing dew. What is "heaven's dew"? Is that perhaps another name for "hidden manna"? It may be! How could we have read our Bible so much and have missed these beautiful descriptions of the things that are eternal - the true riches? Perhaps we were just too preoccupied with earth's richness to notice consistently the refreshing new-every-morning dew of heaven.

How very blessed is the person who is enriched both by heaven's dew and by earth's richness! Yet we must remind ourselves that these two blessings are not at all on a par. The one is temporal; the other is eternal. The one is often measured in monetary terms; the other is priceless. The one is taxable, with ever higher taxation; the other is 100% ours. The one is a mist that appears on the scene of our existence briefly and then evaporates; the other is as solid as the Rock of Ages Himself!

Oh, may it please the Lord to give to us generously of heaven's dew, even as He has so bountifully doled out our portion of earth's richness.

AT MY SIDE

"... the Lord stood at my side and gave me strength."

II Timothy 4:17

Together we have gone through so many things since this physical problem first came to light. I have been by your side, just as in the past when I needed you, you were by my side. Now we <u>both</u> need the Lord to be by our side, giving us strength, and we are pleased to recognize that He <u>is</u> there.

"Surely I will be with you always, to the very end of the age," is the marvelous promise He has made to us. We count upon that promise and that Presence. We have a special need right now for a strong consciousness of His presence.

How wonderful it would be if He would allow us to see Him here in this room with us, the way He did with His disciples after His resurrection. But the fact that our physical eyes cannot see Him does not alter the reality of His presence here any more than our inability to see television waves in this room indicates that they are not here. We simply push a button and proof positive of their presence in our room is suddenly seen on our TV screen. We have no such button that we can push in order to see Jesus who is most certainly here with us, <u>except for a faith button</u>. Even that requires an eyesight that is spiritual rather than physical. Now we see only darkly. Our spiritual eyesight has not matured the way we want it to - not yet, that is!

So, we need continually to remind our hearts that our Lord Jesus is indeed standing at our side, giving us strength. He did it for Paul more than once. He has done it through the ages for His children, and right now, in this very room, He stands by <u>your</u> side to strengthen and encourage you.

"... the Lord stood at my side and gave me strength."

GUARD IT

"I know whom I have believed, and am convinced that He is able to guard what I have entrusted to Him ... Guard the good deposit that was entrusted to you - guard it with the help of the Holy Spirit who lives in us."

II Timothy 1:12,14

The first of these verses is much more familiar than the second, yet they are located only two verses apart in II Timothy! They remind us that while we may be fully convinced that He is able to guard what <u>we</u> have entrusted to <u>Him</u> - we are also to do some guarding ourselves; guarding what <u>He</u> has entrusted to <u>us</u>.

Time and pain and disability would like to become an evil triumvirate capable of snatching away our faith, our hope, our expectation of good things. We must never let that happen. Just as <u>He</u> faithfully guards what we entrust to <u>Him</u>, so <u>we</u> must faithfully guard the promises He has given to <u>us</u>, and the measure of faith He has meted out to us, no matter how small we may perceive that portion to be.

The tiniest bit of living faith (as a grain of mustard seed) can produce marvelous results. We must exercise daily the faith He has given, and strengthen and multiply it through contemplation of His promises. We must remind ourselves that He is faithful in backing those promises. Solomon could say, "There has not failed one word of all His good promises"! We can say that, too, for He has enabled us remarkably and generously during these weeks of confinement. They have slipped by quickly in some ways, and have been filled with serendipitous events that we have enjoyed together. God is good to us. We will guard the things He has taught us and the promises that are so precious to us, with the help of the Holy Spirit.

"He is able to guard what I have entrusted to Him ... Guard the good deposit that was entrusted to you ..."

GOD'S WORK ON DISPLAY

"... this happened so that the work of God might be displayed in his life."   John 9:3

If only we could realize that everything that happens is for a reason! It's easy to ask the question, "Why did this happen to us?" The answer is <u>very</u> explicit here: <u>so that the work of God might be displayed through our lives</u>.

In this specific instance, there was a serious misconception that the Lord Jesus was correcting. A question had just been asked that revealed the theology of the questioners: "Who sinned, this man or his parents?" Jesus made it very clear that their reasoning was on an entirely wrong track. We must never allow Satan to derail us onto that same track.

Our enemy tries to do just that. He uses thoughts like: "With so many people praying, why am I not healed? What is wrong in my life that God is not answering?" That's the same siding on which those people were sitting when the Lord Jesus made it very clear that the purpose was not punitive, but positive. God's work was going to be put on display through this person's condition.

When we offer ourselves to Him for use in a way that will glorify Christ, we don't consciously put in any exclusion clause. Yet, if He chooses to permit illness, we could almost wish that we had! Our human nature shrinks from suffering and pain. That's not a learned reaction - it's instinctive. "Let sorrow do its work; send grief and pain" is a very unnatural prayer! Yet the next thought in those lyrics - "Sweet are Thy messengers, sweet their refrain" is true, even if difficult to comprehend. Our prayer must be, "Please display Your work in our lives, dear Lord!"

"... this happened so that the work of God might be displayed in his life."

GOD IN FRONT!

"... God has gone out in front of you to strike the Philistine army."   I Chronicles 14:15b

When God advances into each new day ahead of us, we do not have to fear. It is a very natural and human response for us to be as fearful as we are at times, but it is not necessary and it is not pleasing to the One who goes before us.

Over in Psalm 68 we also read about God going out before His people. David there rejoiced over that truth. He said that God refreshed His weary people; that He gave them abundant showers of blessing, pouring down rain from Heaven upon them. Then, after describing all that had happened when God went out before His people, he said some things that are so appropriate to our situation. Now, remember, this was after establishing that God goes before His people. He wrote, "Praise be to the Lord, to God, our Savior, who daily bears our burdens. Our God is a God who saves; from the Sovereign LORD comes escape from death. Summon your power, O God; show us your strength, O God, as you have done before ... You are awesome, O God. The God of Israel gives power and strength to His people."

All of these statements, exuding a bold confidence, arise out of the wonderful truth that <u>God goes out before His people</u>. The Israelites had a visible and tangible reminder of God's advance before them, as they watched the cloud by day and the pillar of fire by night. We don't have those, but we can be just as confident, by faith, that He goes before us even in the midst of this physical testing which He has permitted. Let's take comfort in the fact that He goes into each new day ahead of us, and for that reason we shall encounter nothing there that can defeat us.

"...God has gone out in front of you."

GOD CONCERNED?!

"So <u>God</u> looked on the Israelites and <u>was concerned</u> <u>about them</u>."   Exodus 2:25

Translators give great diligence to making sure the wording of their translation conveys the meaning of the original language. In the light of that, this is a most remarkable text!

<u>God</u> ... <u>concerned</u>? That's amazing! If it had said, "God cared about them," that would be different. "Concerned" has a connotation almost synonymous with "worried," yet we cannot imagine God worrying about anything. He has nothing to worry about, but He does have things with which to concern Himself. So, there appears to be a difference between worry and concern.

We must never forget that God looks with concern upon your pain, whether it is physical pain or the pain of confinement and weakness. He knows how you are feeling in the midst of this severe trial. His purpose in allowing this we do not readily understand, but His unfailing love we do not have to question. God _is_ concerned about us. He watches over us lovingly to make certain His basic principle is not violated ... that is, that He is not testing us beyond what we are able to endure. "God keeps faith, and He will not allow you to be tested above your powers, but when the test comes, He will at the same time provide a way out, by enabling you to sustain it." (I Cor. 10:13 N.E.B.) "Father-filtered!" a radio speaker exclaimed. Right! Nothing gets to us without being Father-filtered. Yes, He _is_ concerned about us both.

"So God looked on the Israelites and was concerned about them."

GOD DISTRESSED!

"In all their distress, <u>He too was distressed</u>."

Isaiah 63:9

Here is another passage that speaks of God in a manner that is difficult for us to comprehend. In our last devotional we noticed that God is <u>concerned</u> about us (Exodus 2:25). Even <u>that</u> word selection made us stop and think. <u>Distressed</u> is an even stronger word. It is difficult for us to think of God as being distressed.

Yet we can remember that the Lord Jesus stood by the grave of Lazarus and <u>wept</u>! We can also recall that we have been told we can <u>grieve</u> the Holy Spirit. God <u>does</u> have the same emotions that we have. He feels with us in an empathy incomparable. People often sympathize with us. We don't like that. We don't really want anyone's sympathy. Something deep within us finds that distasteful - almost repulsive. Empathizing is quite another thing.

When we meet someone who is going through the

same struggle we are facing, we feel an immediate closeness and bonding of spirit. There is no sympathizing; there is a beautiful empathizing instead. Sympathy represents "feeling sorry for." Empathy means "to feel with." "Your pain in my heart," someone has beautifully defined it.

I think that is a good description of what the Lord is talking about here. "In all their distress he too was distressed." That's Divine empathy. How amazing that our pain is in His heart! He suffers along with us.

Then, why does He permit it, when He has the power to stop it? If I could, I would take away every pain from you. He can, and He doesn't. He has His reasons. We must trust, submitting to His timing, and finding comfort in knowing He feels with us - deeply.

"In all their distress, He too was distressed."

FORTY YEARS!

"For forty years you sustained them; ... they lacked nothing." Nehemiah 9:21

We too can look back upon many wonderful years during which God has directed our lives precisely and beautifully; years during which we were Divinely sustained. Our hearts are filled with praise for His faithfulness to us. We, too, have "lacked nothing". Our finances have been taken care of generously and at times even miraculously. Our opportunities to serve Him have been blessed by Him wonderfully. Our footsteps have been ordered by Him through every circumstance of our lives, both pleasant and unpleasant, good and bad, joyful and sorrowful.

We have survived emotionally draining family situations that were threatening to inundate us. He sustained us. We have plodded together through physical distresses and emotional upheavals. Always He was there to sustain us. In good years and in bad God has continued to sustain us faithfully. We can

114

say with joy and deep appreciation that we have lacked nothing.

He will continue to sustain us. "This God is our God for ever and ever; He will be our Guide even to the end." We must not forget that for many years He has guided us together. Before that He guided us separately, preparing us for each other. He certainly will not stop now.

We will trust God to sustain us throughout this trial, bringing it to a victorious conclusion as He has all other trials during these many years. We shall continue to lack nothing. He will give grace for our trials, strength for our weakness, and encouragement when we are in need of it. All of these will be our portion as our Great Sustainer continues to make certain that we, too, "lack nothing."

"For forty years you sustained them ... they lacked nothing."

FOR THIS - JESUS!

"This calls for <u>patient endurance</u> and faithfulness on the part of the saints." "This calls for <u>patient endurance</u> on the part of the saints who obey God's commands and remain faithful to Jesus."   Revelation 13:10c; 14:12

Here we have two challenging reminders directed toward people who are going through severe trials. They tie in so beautifully with a comforting statement that has appeared in print anonymously: "<u>For this I have Jesus</u>!" Each concept enables the other. If we keep reminding ourselves in the midst of the trials of life that, "For this I have Jesus," we will be able to "patiently endure," and to "remain faithful to Jesus" in spite of those trials.

So, there are two thoughts it would be advisable to memorize for the difficult times which may yet be ahead for each of us. First: "This calls for patient endurance and faithfulness" and secondly, "For this I have Jesus."

What a good balance! The first reminds us of what

we are to do, while the second reminds us of what He will do. Perhaps the two are closely related. As we patiently endure, He gives of Himself all we have need of. He provides strength and grace, fulfilling His promise that His grace is sufficient for us and His strength is perfected in the midst of our weakness.

"He giveth more grace when the burdens grow greater;
  He sendeth more strength when the labors increase.
   To added affliction, He addeth His mercy,
    To multiplied trials, His multiplied peace.
 When we have exhausted our store of endurance,
   When our strength has failed
    Ere the day is half done,
      When we reach the end of our hoarded resources,
       Our Father's full giving is only begun.
 His love has no limit, His grace has no measure,
  His power has no boundary known unto men;
    For out of His infinite riches in Jesus,
      He giveth, and giveth, and giveth again!"

117

DON'T BE ANXIOUS

"Do not be anxious about anything, but in everything, by prayer and petition, with thanksgiving, present your requests to God." Philippians 4:6

Anxiety can exact a heavy toll from us if we are not careful. It is only natural to be anxious when things are not going well. When we are faced with uncertainties about what is wrong and what the outcome will be, anxiety is an almost unavoidable by-product.

So, when God tells us not to be anxious, He has to give the enabling or we simply cannot obey His command. He must grant to us the peace that passes understanding or we will spontaneously worry.

The alternative to worry offered here is prayer and petition with thanksgiving. We <u>have</u> prayed. We <u>have</u> petitioned God, presenting our earnest prayers to Him over and over. We <u>have</u> offered our thanksgiving. I recall how many, many times you have said the words, "I just can't thank the Lord

enough for strengthening me to be able to do this!"
We have done what God through Paul urged, and
now we can "stand still and see the salvation of the
Lord." Encouragements have certainly come to us,
but not the big deliverance we have been asking for -
not yet.

In connection with this uplifting verse, a beautiful
gospel song comes to mind. First, let's repeat the
verse. "Do not be anxious about anything, but in
everything, by prayer and petition, with
thanksgiving, present your requests to God." Now
the song:

"All your anxiety, all your care,

Bring to the Mercy-seat, leave it there.

Never a burden that He cannot bear,

Never a Friend like Jesus."

In response to this encouragement, we bring to the
Mercy-seat our anxiety and cares and we place them
there, trusting our incomparable Friend.   *

CONTINUAL SURVEILLANCE

"From heaven the LORD *looks down and sees all mankind; from His dwelling place He watches all who live on earth - He who forms the hearts of all, who considers everything they do."* Psalm 33:13-15

This is a powerful truth. Unfortunately it has been used to threaten God's people with the emphasis being placed upon God seeing every evil deed of man. Though that is the truth, and it certainly is a deterrent from evil, it is much more encouraging to apply this truth to our needs and the happy recognition that we are continually observed and protected by our loving Lord. He watches over us, and He considers everything we do. David expressed it so forcefully in the 139th Psalm:

"O LORD, you have searched me and you know me. You know when I sit down and when I rise ... You discern my going out and my lying down; You are familiar with all my ways. Before a word is on my tongue, you know it completely ... When I was woven together ... your eyes saw my unformed body. All the days ordained for me were written in your book before one of them came to be ... How precious ..."

Such omniscience is both staggering to the mind <u>and</u> comforting. Nothing <u>ever</u> escapes the notice of God. He knows our every need and in His great love He comes to our rescue. Based upon previous experience, it is not unrealistic for us to expect great and mighty things from our loving, all-powerful God.

In our bad moments as well as in our good ones (<u>but especially when things are not going well</u>) we need to remember the encouraging truths set forth in these three verses, reminding ourselves that God has not lost control - <u>and He never will</u>!

"From heaven the LORD looks down and sees all mankind; from His dwelling place He watches all who live on earth - He who forms the hearts of all, who considers everything they do."

CAN GOD?

"Can God spread a table in the desert? When he (Moses) struck the rock, water gushed out, and streams flowed abundantly. But can He also give us food? Can He supply meat for His people?"   Psalm 78:19,20

What foolish questions! The God who could make water gush from a rock can <u>surely</u> provide <u>anything</u> else a person needs, including meat for His people.

We need assistance in realizing that <u>anything</u> we have need of is within His power to provide - <u>absolutely anything</u>. We know that God has no limitations. Intellectually we know that, but because we <u>do</u> have limitations (lots of them), it is difficult for us to comprehend an existence where there is nothing impossible. It is a world very foreign to ours; a beautiful, wonderful world where <u>God</u> feels completely comfortable, even if <u>we</u> don't!

It is good for us to reminisce, recalling all the marvelous things God has done for us from time to time that went beyond what we could have expected.

To the Israelites at one point God said, "I will be to you a God and you shall <u>know</u> that I am the Lord your God!" God loves to manifest Himself to His children. He wants to be very real to us. He wants to answer prayers for us, and make us <u>know</u> that He is the Lord, our God.

For us personally such certainty is His desire and purpose. We must never be found in the company of the doubters, but must firmly take our place among those who dare to believe that the God who has already done so much has no limitations whatsoever. Yes, <u>God can</u> provide for His people absolutely anything they need. He has proven that to us repeatedly. When we remember all He has already done, we rejoice. This simple little chorus sums it all up:

> "God is so good,
>> He answers prayer,
>> We love Him so,
>>> He's so good to us."

BE STILL

"Do not be afraid. Stand firm and you will see the deliverance the LORD will bring you today. The Egyptians you see today you will never see again. The LORD will fight for you; you need only to be still."

"You need only to be still." There's a sweet, quiet power inherent in confident stillness that the world knows nothing about, primarily because it knows nothing about the nature of God. Our times are bustling, brash, and brazenly boisterous. Consequently, we are not as familiar with the "Blessed Quietness" spoken of in one of our Gospel songs as we could be. The evil triumvirate of Hurry, Worry, and Flurry are much better known, and certainly more popular.

"Be still and know that I am God," the Psalmist, Korah wrote. And so beautifully the twentieth century Psalmist, Mrs. Hal Buckner, expressed it:

"That He is God, be still and know,
  Though storm-swept be your weary soul,
    Your deepest grief to Him is woe,
    And over all He has control.
  Though shattered hopes surround you still,
    Though dark and rugged is your way,
      Know this: for you a Father's will,
        Preordains all things day by day.
  No depth of storm nor strength of gale,
    Can move you from your place secure;
      His power o'er these shall still prevail,
        His boundless love shall still endure.
  Be still and know, be still and know,
    That He is God, ...be still and know.
      He sees and feels your deepest woe,
        That He is God, be still and know."

There is a profound beauty and inconceivable strength in the simple admonition, "You do not need to be afraid ... stand firm ... you need only to be still."

A TESTIMONY

"Jethro was delighted to hear about all the good things the LORD had done ... He said, 'Praise be to the LORD, who rescued you ...'"   Exodus 18:9a,10a

God has done good things for us, too. We must give Him praise for that at every opportunity. "Praise is beautiful," the Bible tells us. It has an effect on our own well-being as well as upon those who hear that praise.

Our testimony to the Lord's goodness can elicit praise from the hearts of others. We must be careful to give God the glory for the answers to prayer that come so regularly.

I think we do. The letters that we send to our friends spell out the wonderful answers to prayer that we have from time to time, and that rewards them for praying. They can feel they have had a part in each victory, and rightly so, for <u>they have</u>!

When we have accomplished something that turns out well, we do enjoy the praises of others (it is only human to want affirmation like that). But perhaps there is something Divine about it as well, for we are instructed to offer our praises to God for all <u>His</u> wondrous works. Gladly we respond with our praises. He has done so much for us, not only in giving some really good days, but also in giving grace for the bad ones. Both glorify Him.

Let's look for every opportunity to elicit praise from others for the Lord's goodness, as we give testimony to His grace, and show openly His Divine interventions that have made such a difference.

Jesus said of one person's illness that it was so that God would be glorified. And God was, <u>through the man's healing</u>. Your illness can bring glory to God. <u>It already has</u>. We want deliverance, but we also want all His glorious purposes fulfilled.

"Jethro was delighted to hear about all the good things the LORD had done ... He said, 'Praise be to the LORD, who rescued you ...'"

A SETTLED MIND

"... all who fear God and trust in Him are blessed beyond expression. ... (they do) not fear bad news, nor live in dread of what may happen. For (they) are settled in (their) mind(s) that Jehovah will take care of (them)."

Psalm 112:1,7 (L.B.)

It is our wonderful privilege to put fear and dread aside and to rest peacefully in the sublime confidence that Jehovah will take care of us. Having heard the possibilities from one doctor after another, it is not humanly possible to live without fear and dread; but it is Divinely possible!

The only fear we need have as Christians is the fear of the Lord, and that is a profitable one. He is a caring Father who does for His children lovingly all that is needed. He will not let us down. In our hearts we know that.

It is our enemy who is the author of fear. Perfect love casts out fear, and we have in our loving Father the only example of perfect love that exists. We will put our future in His hands and refuse to fear no matter how dark the various prognoses may be.

It would be most revealing to have a long list made for us of all the things that have never happened that we have feared in our lifetime. We certainly do a lot of unnecessary worrying! Now, when we must trust more than we have ever been called upon to trust before, we need to remember that the Lord will indeed take care of us in every aspect of our lives. He always has; He always will.

The provision of the Lord for us has been bountiful. We look back with great appreciation on all the good things He has showered upon us. We have had a fruitful, enjoyable life and ministry. This is certainly not the time to begin to fear bad news, nor to "live in dread of what may happen." We just won't do that! *"... all who fear and trust in Him are blessed beyond expression. ... they do not fear bad news, nor live in dread of what may happen. For they are settled in their mind that Jehovah will take care of them."*

A PREPARED PLACE

"I am going ... to prepare a place for you. And if I go and prepare a place for you, I will come back and take you to be with Me that you also may be with Me where I am."   John 14:2,3

How ever can our earth-bound imaginations rise to picture in any adequate manner the place the Lord Jesus is preparing for us? It must be beautiful beyond our wildest imaginations. He has had two thousand years to perfect it with details that are so extravagantly elegant that we could never conceive of them.

Even now the most impressive things on earth are not man-made, but are the wonders of "nature." The roaring falls of Niagara, and Iguazu, and Victoria cause man to stand in unbridled awe. The grandeur of the well-named Grand Canyon cannot be told - it must be experienced. The marvel of El Altar and Cayambe and Sangai in their towering majesty as they scrape the skies of Ecuador cannot be adequately described to others. The miles and miles of tulips in Holland, the carpet of grapes along the Rhine, the grandeur of the Yungfrau or Mount Pilatus in Switzerland - all of these are God-made, not man-made. They are only prototypes of what we shall experience and take delight in when we see what He has prepared for us up there.

Far better than all of this will be the enjoyment of being with Him whom our souls adore. What an ecstacy of joy that will be!

You may precede me there, my sweetheart. For you it will be far more than a release from this frail body. It will be a glorious rendezvous with Him whom your soul has loved deeply. Someday I shall join you there. Together we will contemplate the wonders of His handiwork as we have done here, but on a far grander scale. Together we will worship the One who gave us life abundantly.   *

A PRABLE MINISTRY

"After Job had prayed for his friends, the LORD made him prosperous again and gave him twice as much as he had before."   Job 42:10

Confinement because of illness can leave you feeling so useless, especially since you were so active for the Lord in earlier days. Your prayer ministry, however, cannot be taken from you except if your mental capacity is impaired. God has graciously not allowed that, so you still have your daily quiet time when you minister to others through prayer.

What a ministry that is! How far-reaching! You can even participate in our pastor's sermon preparations through prayer. You can be a help to our friends who are passing through similar dark valleys, even when they are far removed from us geographically. You can be effective on the various mission fields of the earth - in Russia, Africa, South America, Japan (customize by naming countries where missionaries you know are ministering).   The world is your parish - the whole wide world! This severe trial of yours cannot stop that.

The temptation is to feel that all opportunities for serving the Lord have been taken away from you. <u>That is not so</u>. In addition to a prayer ministry, you minister by your cheerful spirit when friends drop by to visit. It is so obvious that you are in victory, in the midst of the most severe trial of your life.

Evident victory like that is a forceful testimony to the sustaining power of our living Lord. No, your ministry is <u>not</u> over; it has changed. You have been given more time to pray.

"After Job had prayed for his friends, the LORD made him prosperous again and gave him twice as much as he had before."

ALWAYS ON TOP

"If you pay attention to the commands of the LORD your God ... and carefully follow them, you will <u>always</u> be <u>at the top</u>, never at the bottom."   Deuteronomy 28:13

What an unusual promise! A careful following of the Lord's commands guarantees always being on top of things. There are times when this promise needs to be remembered and claimed.

Every Christian feels at times as if the bottom has fallen out of things, and that he was in it when it did. Yet, the Lord is here promising that we will "always be at the top."

The provisions that have been made for victorious handling of the trials of life are fabulous. We have not been promised exemption from trials, but we surely have been promised victory in the midst of those problem times.

But there is an "if" with which this wonderful verse begins: "If you pay attention to the commands of the Lord your God ... and carefully follow them." That's where the hitch comes. We are not meticulously consistent in following His commands, so we do not have really consistent victory.

God has promised to keep us in perfect peace, providing our minds remain fixed upon Him. Our tendency is to become so overwhelmed by the immediate trial that our minds are inundated with the details of the problem instead of being transfixed upon the Lord who made the wonderful promise. So - we lose that "perfect peace" He promised and provided.

God assures us that careful following of His commands will keep us always on top. We must remember this the next time we are tempted to take up even temporary residence "under the circumstances." That is no place for a Christian to so much as linger!

"If you pay attention to the commands of the LORD your God ...and carefully follow them, you will always be at the top, never at the bottom."

ALL THINGS NEW

"He who was seated on the throne said, 'I am making everything new!'" *"... I will create new heavens and a new earth."* Revelation 21:5; Isaiah 65:17

There is a strong desire within our hearts for the return of our Savior and the fulfillment of these prophecies. We see life and the world differently from vivacious, healthy young people who have their full strength and vitality and who have great plans for the future.

Many of life's baubles have lost their bubble. Earth's pleasures have faded and jaded and will probably never be quite the same again. On the one hand, this loss of the pleasure capacity <u>can</u> be a sign of depression, but on the other hand, it is decidedly a part of growing older. Hearing and sight and taste buds and glands all change and along with those changes, the colorfulness of life itself gradually fades.

As these pleasures diminish, others become brighter! The prospect of Christ's imminent return becomes more welcome and alluring. The thought of everything being made new becomes most appealing. Both Old and New Testaments contain this promise that all things will be made new, though the wording differs. In Revelation we read, "I am making everything new." In Isaiah we hear God say, "I will create new heavens and a new earth." Before God sent the Lord Jesus to this sin-cursed earth, He had in mind the new-making of it. First He would new-make us, and then He would provide a newly made place for us to enjoy. To the exciting promise of new heavens and a new earth we may reasonably add: and new bodies, new dwelling places, new celestial air to breathe, a new keenness of understanding, and all kinds of other new things that are appealing. Oh, please hasten that day, dear Lord!

"He who was seated on the throne said, 'I am making everything new!'" *"... I will create new heavens and a new earth."*

A HEART AT PEACE

"A heart at peace gives life to the body ..."

Proverbs 14:30

God has given us an amazing peace and contentment in the midst of our trial. What a wonderful gift! We have remarked about it more than once to others and to each other.

This verse reveals a side-effect of the heart that enjoys a God-given peace. <u>Life itself</u> is said to be a by-product. God's medications and stimulants to health are so different from man's. In another verse God says that a merry heart is good medicine. Here we are told that a peaceful heart gives life to the body.

So then, anything that strengthens our sense of peace, or brings rejoicing to our hearts becomes a powerful medicine and good therapy, above and beyond what medical science attempts to do.

The peacefulness of heart God has given is a wonderful gift, and we do appreciate it deeply. Shut in from the fields of air, we are, yet we don't fret or chafe. We just sit here in our little cage and sing of Him who placed us here, as a canary in its confined area chooses to fill the house with bird song.

We are encouraged by this text to realize that new life can come to your body by way of this peacefulness of heart and soul. It really does make sense. It is the antithesis of the way stress brings on disease. The body is <u>weakened</u> by stress, but <u>strengthened</u> by peace. Stress <u>opens</u> the door for disease; peace <u>closes</u> it.

Can peace and sorrows live together? Amazingly, yes! "When peace like a river attendeth my way; when sorrows like seabillows roll," H. G. Spafford wrote after his four daughters had drowned. It <u>is</u> possible to have peace even "when sorrows like seabillows roll." Our prayer should be for hearts that continue at peace.

"A heart at peace gives life to the body ..."

AGAIN AND AGAIN

"The LORD ... sent word to them through His messengers <u>*again and again*</u>*, because He had pity on His people ... "*

II Chronicles 36:15

God takes note of <u>us</u>, too, in <u>our</u> troubled condition. He takes pity on us, and sends word of His loving interest. Again and again He sends "messengers" who are His servants, acting out of <u>their</u> love, but also prompted by <u>His</u> love.

People who care have sent us so many cards and notes. They have selected them carefully and they want them to be a comfort and blessing to us.

It's easy to read them quickly and go on to the next one, without allowing the message that was <u>sent by the Lord through His messengers</u> to become the blessing it was intended to be.

We must read our cards more slowly and thoughtfully. The Scripture verses, though familiar, must be savored. The poetry, though sometimes trite, must be allowed to do the work intended. The love of the person sending the card must be allowed to flow freely through that expression of loving concern.

Let's take a different approach to the incoming mail the next few days. You open and read the card first. Then I will read it aloud to you, as we attempt to extract every bit of sweetness and encouragement from it we possibly can. The cards and phone calls that come to us so regularly are indeed <u>words from our loving Lord coming through messengers that He is prompting</u> to carry His words of encouragement.

Let's look forward to that next card or phone call and receive it as another of His "again and again" dispatched expressions of loving concern.

"The LORD ... sent word to them through His messengers again and again, because He had pity on His people ..."

ABSOLUTE SOVEREIGNTY

"Exactly as I say it I have it happen. Just as I plan I do it." Isaiah 46:11b (Beck)

There is no equivocating here. God is saying that things happen in conjunction with His sovereignty - His <u>absolute</u> sovereignty. There is great comfort in that.

We are both immortal until what God has planned for us to do is completed. And even when we reach that point, it is an exciting one, for then we begin the next incomparably glorious phase of our eternal existence. So, the clever statement we have heard so often, "A person is immortal until his life's work is done," is only a half-truth. A true Christian is in one sense immortal eternally for we shall never die other than the death that is a part of this temporary, fleeting life. God is in complete control. He is in control of this day. He will be in control not only of tomorrow, but also of all our tomorrows. We have nothing to fear. The doctors expect you to precede me into the next beautiful and perfect phase of our eternal life in Christ. Only God knows if they are right.

The fact of the matter is that the way time is flying, soon we will both be enjoying a freedom we never knew here. I fully expect to share it with you in every aspect. We have loved to travel here and I think we shall enjoy it even more there, for there will be no Miami to frighten us there. There will be no long layovers for the next plane. There will be no language barriers. There will be no weariness or weakness. There will be no thieves to fear, and no bad roads to distress.

Yes, there's a great day coming for both of us. We need not speculate about when or how, for God has said this, "Exactly as I say it, I have it happen. Just as I plan, I do it." We rest in that.

SURE FOUNDATION

"He will be the <u>sure foundation</u> for your times ... the fear of the LORD is the key to this treasure."   Isaiah 33:6

Our foot could so easily slip on this difficult path the Lord has included in our earth-experience except that He Himself provides a sure footing. We have never walked this way before, and we find all kinds of new and treacherous aspects of the footpath. Though <u>we</u> have never traversed this path before, <u>He</u> has!

"He knows the way that (we) take..." is a very comforting statement made by one whose path was rougher than ours. (Job!)

"A sure foundation for (our) times" is a wonderful promise. These are the times that try our faith and our depth as Christians more than any preceding time. Yet in the midst of them there is a treasure to be found, and then added to our already great store.

"The fear of the Lord is the key to this treasure." Isaiah says. We do have a deep respect for our Lord. We admire His limitless power and know He can use it on our behalf in a moment. We stand in awe of His great holiness and thank Him for imputing righteousness to us as well, through His Son. We marvel at the vastness of His wisdom and trust Him to do what is right for us. We thrill to remember that He works all things together for the good of the ones who love Him. We look forward to the unveiling of His plan so we can see why we were asked to walk this path of pain.

These are painful times. These are difficult times. Yet they are also times when we can give testimony to His sustaining grace and power, for He enables us to handle one day at a time in victory.

Our feet will not slip! <u>We have a sure foundation</u>!

"He will be the sure foundation for your times ... the fear of the LORD is the key to this treasure."

"As the deer pants for streams of water, so my soul pants for You, O God. My soul thirsts for God, for the living God. ... My tears have been my food day and night ... These things I remember as I pour out my soul: how I used to go (out with other people) ... with joy and thanksgiving.

Why are you downcast, O my soul? Why so disturbed within me? Put your hope in God, for I will yet praise Him, my Savior and my God.

By day the Lord directs His love, at night His song is with me - a prayer to the God of my life.

... Why are you downcast, O my soul? Why so disturbed within me? Put your hope in God, for I will yet praise Him, my Savior and my God.

You are ... my stronghold. Why must I ... mourn? ... Send forth Your light and Your truth, let them guide me; let them bring me to Your mountain, to the place where You dwell. Then will I (find God to be) ... my joy and my delight. I will praise You, ... O God, my God.

Why are you downcast, O my soul? Why so disturbed within me? Put your hope in God, for I will yet praise Him, my Savior and my God. Psalm 42, 43

"Don't give up hope," fellow Christians urge us from time to time. That's good advice. Our hope is in God, and we need to be reminded of that. We shall yet praise Him. He has brought us this far through the "valley of the shadow of death" and we must not forget the miracles He has already wrought. There is nothing impossible with God.

We must repeatedly ask ourselves the question asked three times in these two Psalms: "Why are you downcast, O my soul? Why so disturbed within me?" We must place our hope in God, confident that we will yet praise Him, for He is our Savior and our God.

VAST RESOURCES

"I ask the God of our Lord Jesus Christ, the Father of glory, to give you His Spirit to ... reveal the truth to you as you learn to know Him better and to enlighten the eyes of your mind so that you may know ... <u>the vast resources of His power</u> working in us who believe. It is the same mighty power ... which ... raised (Christ) from the dead ..." Eph. 1:17-20 (Beck)

The words, "the vast resources of His power" are encouraging ones. There is <u>nothing</u> our Lord cannot do. All the things that concern us, in <u>every</u> area, can be brought to the One who has "vast resources of power," and left there.

Those in our family for whom we are concerned are so thoroughly known to Him. He is able to bring salvation, deliverance, added strength, healing, and enablings, according to the specific need of each of them in answer to our prayers. "Oh, for a faith that will not shrink though pressed by many a foe, that will not tremble on the brink of any (of these) earthly woes."

148

Our prayer has to be simply, "Lord, give us such a faith as this"! We are not able to manufacture it. It has to be a gift from our Lord Jesus, who is "the Author and Perfecter of our faith."

It will not be the first time He has given us a faith we could not have exercised on our own. At our salvation the faith to believe was "the gift of God;" it was "not of ourselves." Remember that passage? "By grace you have been saved, through faith - and this (faith) not from yourselves, it is the gift of God - not by works so that no one can boast." (Ephesians 2:8,9)

That God-given faith made us alive in the first place, eternally. Now we must trust Him for more God-given faith that will keep us alive here and productive for Him. He has vast resources of power with which to do anything and everything we need.   *

VALLEY OF WEEPING

"Happy are those who are strong in the Lord, who want above all else to follow Your steps. When they walk through the <u>Valley of Weeping</u> it will become a place of springs where pools of blessing and refreshment collect after rains! They will grow constantly in strength and each of them is invited to meet with the Lord ..."

Psalm 84:5-7a (L.B.)

What beautiful things are said about the "Valley of Weeping"! It is not pictured here as a dark, forbidding valley from which we instinctively shrink back, and out of which we are desperate to climb.

<u>Blessing</u>, <u>refreshment</u>, <u>strength</u>, and <u>fellowship</u> are all mentioned as profitable adjuncts of tears. That's a perspective we don't readily grasp, because it is quite contrary to what we have set our hearts upon. We only welcome weeping when the tears are tears of joy. That's a very human trait.

Even the Psalmist associates weeping with the night and joy with the morning when he reminds us that "weeping may last through the night, but joy comes in the morning."

The Psalmist does call the place of weeping a "valley," but he insists that it is a <u>profitable</u> valley.

He speaks of pools of refreshment and blessing, as well as of constant growth in strength. Then comes the apex of all of the benefits: an invitation to meet with the Lord! The contents of these three verses are almost beyond our grasp. A victory over weeping is depicted here that is so beautiful it seems almost unreal. Actually, it <u>is</u> unreal, except to the true Christian. The people of the world know nothing about this kind of victory, for they don't know the Lord who has made all these "Valley of Weeping" blessings possible.

"Happy are those who are strong in the Lord ... The <u>Valley of Weeping</u> will become a place of springs where pools of blessing and refreshment collect after rains! They will grow constantly in strength and each of them is invited to meet with the Lord ..."

TRUST!

"You will keep in perfect peace him whose mind is steadfast, because he trusts in You. Trust in the LORD forever, for the LORD, the LORD, is the Rock eternal."

Isaiah 26:3,4

Our trustworthy Lord has never given us reason to doubt Him. He has through the years fulfilled one promise after another to us, and given us a strong foundation of experience to justify an implicit trust.

By contrast, our doctors have blundered more than once. Their failures and misdiagnoses were not deliberate. They were a reflection of the imperfection of man, and a reminder that our basic faith has to be placed in God and not in the medical profession, or in man's limited knowledge.

Perfect peace is the result of perfect trust, and we must learn more and more thoroughly how to trust. Trust comes easily to a child. As we grow older and our trust is betrayed, we find it increasingly difficult to trust. We need to be children of the Heavenly Father, praying sincerely:

"Lord keep me trusting Thee day after day,
Trusting whatever befall on my way;
Sunshine or shadow, I take them from Thee,
Knowing Thy grace is sufficient for me.
Trusting Thee more! Trusting Thee more!
May every day find me trusting Thee more.
Cares may surround me, and clouds hover o'er,
But keep me, Lord Jesus, still trusting Thee more."

It must bring pleasure to the heart of God when we rest trustfully in Him rather than fretting over the circumstances in which we find ourselves. Trust proclaims confidently that we know He does what is best for His children, and that He permits no trial or sorrow that is not profitable in some special way. Yes, the Lord, _our_ Lord, is a Rock eternal, and on Christ, the Solid Rock we stand, knowing well that all other ground is sinking sand. We _will_ trust, and we _will_ have perfect peace.   *

SUMMER AND WINTER

"You made both summer and winter."   Psalm 74:17b

How different summertime is from wintertime! During the one we resort to air-conditioning to remain comfortable. During the other we pay high fuel bills for the same purpose. During the one we watch things grow, and during the other we wait for them to start growing again. There are <u>so</u> many contrasts.

In life there are summertimes and wintertimes, too. We are currently enduring one of our more severe "winters." So are some of our friends. We must be faithful in asking God to help them as they pass through their bitterly cold winters.

As severe as our own "winter" is currently, we recognize that there are those who have a worse storm that they are trying to weather. We have been able to stay above depression, with a special enabling the Lord Himself has given. That in itself is no small gift! Looking back, we remember the summertimes the

Lord has given us repeatedly during our lifetime together. Now, though we cannot "enjoy" this wintertime, <u>we can keep warm</u> by immersing ourselves in the wonderful promises of His Word and by reminding our hearts of His loving faithfulness to us. We must never forget that our God is in complete control. "He knows the way we take, and when we come forth we shall be as gold," Job said. It will be gold that has been refined by the fire, pure and precious and pleasing to the Lord.

"<u>Summer and winter</u>, and springtime and harvest,
   Sun, moon, and stars in their courses above,
     Join with all nature in manifold witness
       To Thy great faithfulness, mercy and love."

Yes, great is Thy faithfulness, Maker of both summer and winter!

SPARROW CARE

"Are not two <u>sparrows</u> sold for a penny? Yet <u>not one of</u> <u>them will fall to the ground apart from the will of your</u> <u>Father.</u> And even the very hairs of your head are all numbered. So don't be afraid; you are worth more than many sparrows."   Matthew 10:29,30

God's detailed oversight of the world He created is incredible to us limited and very finite mortals. There are birds deep in the jungles of South America that no human eye has ever seen. In the great forests of our own land are birds and animals that He not only designed originally, but also knows all about today. He sees when they fall - <u>every one</u>! That is beyond our ability to comprehend, but it <u>is</u> true.

We even find it difficult to understand how God can simultaneously hear thousands of prayers. Right now, as we meditate together, hearts and voices are being raised to God from everywhere on the entire earth. Some are facing a new day, having their morning devotions. Simultaneously, others are closing their day with prayer. Some are in hospital lounges, anxiously awaiting the surgeon's appearance, hoping for good news. While they wait, they are crying out to God to guide the hand that holds the scalpel.

Every imaginable prayer scenario is more than likely being enacted right at this moment. In His unlimited knowledge, God hears it all, <u>every</u> prayer. That's difficult for us to imagine in spite of the fact that man does a similar thing when he sends 150,000 messages simultaneously over a fiber optic strand. In our one, poorly used brain, we store a staggering amount of data in a lifetime - we know that. We don't understand all these things, but we <u>do</u> know God, and we know that we are currently benefiting from His hearing <u>our</u> prayers. Since God commits Himself to sparrow-care, He surely cares deeply about the apex of His creation!

"So don't be afraid; you are worth more than many sparrows."

DELAYED RESPONSE

"... Since the first day ... your prayers were heard, and I have come in response to them. But the prince of the Persian kingdom <u>resisted</u> me <u>twenty-one days</u>. Then Michael, one of the chief princes, came to help me, because I was detained there ... "   Daniel 10:12

This passage gives us an insight into the spiritual warfare that goes on in unseen places. In the previous chapter the angel said to Daniel, "As soon as you began to pray an answer was given." We too need a strong realization that as soon as we begin to pray our prayers are heard and an answer is given. We do not always receive it immediately, but it is given right away, so we need to act with an assurance that the answer is on the way.

In this instance a three-week delay must have seemed like a <u>very</u> long time to Daniel who was praying so earnestly, and waiting. There have been times when we've become weary in praying for something, as there seems to be no answer forthcoming.

The temptation is to wonder whether we have been heard. <u>Oh</u>, <u>yes</u>, <u>we have</u>! Our prayer <u>is heard</u> immediately, and an answer <u>is given</u> immediately as well, even though it is common for us to have a delay in the receiving of that answer to prayer.

These delays are similar to what we experience with our mail systems around the world. For example, to get an answer from a letter directed to Canada, I would expect about three weeks to pass, even if the person answered my letter promptly. And <u>that</u> is without Satanic opposition! The answers to our prayers are deliberately thwarted by the forces of evil, so we must learn to pray with both persistence and patience.

"... Since the first day ... your prayers were heard ... but ... I was detained ..."

SO MUCH!

"Oh, ... God has given you so much. ... He took you as His own ... and led you along ... and told you how very much He wanted to bless you. He gave you His rules for daily life so you would know what He wanted you to do. He let you worship Him, and gave you mighty promises ... Praise God forever!"   Romans 9:1-5 (L.B.)

Yes, God has given us <u>so much</u>! We look back over our lives and our hearts overflow with praise, for God has richly blessed us in so many ways through all our years.

Life has not always been rosy. We have had domestic heartaches, financial concerns, physical distresses, church problems, and our share of tears. Through all of those burdens, so heavy to bear, we have had the Lord. We have had each other. We have had friends who have stood by us faithfully. We have had His mighty promises.

Yes, God has given us <u>so</u> much! Not the least of His wonderful gifts have been the "mighty promises" mentioned in this passage. How tenaciously we have clung to them all through this current struggle. Looking back we marvel at what has happened. God has done some phenomenal things. Looking to the present, we in fear and trembling reach out our hands, praying they will be filled by Him with yet another miracle that is obviously of His doing.

We have lived through this together, drawing what we have needed month by month, week by week, even day by day, and finding a sufficient supply of grace for even the darkest hours.

Our hearts are full of praise, and rightly so. These have been times of proving the sufficiency of His grace to endure suffering and the onslaughts of the enemy. Despite all kinds of reverses, we always seem to come back out into the sunlight again, by His enabling. Yes, "God has given (us) so much. Praise God forever!"

SHARE IN MY TROUBLES

"... it was good of you to share in my troubles."
Philippians 4:14

Paul wrote these words to the Philippians. We could write them to so many people who through prayer, giving, phoning, and sending flowers and other gifts have shared in <u>our</u> troubles!

Whenever we feel about to slip under a wave of depression, along comes a long-distance phone call, or a local gift of food, or the florist's truck with an expression of love, or a friend with a beautiful, sweet-smelling rose. People seem to be led of God at the very moment we need it to <u>share in our troubles</u>.

No matter how deep or dark our valley becomes, we must pray that God will give us the excess energy to be able to share in the troubles of others. We want no day to pass by without our fulfilling our determination to reach out and touch someone daily with love. We have no difficulty finding the people who need it; we just need God's help in maintaining the ability to look beyond our own "giants" to see the ones other people are facing. There are moments when our "giants" tower over us so tall and huge that they almost block out our view of others. So far that has not happened, and we must pray that it never will.

The giants that Caleb and Joshua saw when they scouted out the promised land were the same ones that the other ten spies saw. The big difference was that "others saw the giants; Caleb saw the Lord." As long as our view of God does not dim, we shall have the ability not only to continue on in faith, but also to reach out in His love to others who are hurting and need a word of encouragement, so they can say of us, "It was good of <u>you</u> to <u>share in my troubles</u>."

REJOICE ALWAYS

"... you are to <u>rejoice</u> before the LORD your God <u>in</u> everything you put your hand to." Deuteronomy 12:18b

How very like Philippians 4:4 this sounds: "Rejoice in the Lord always. I will say it again: Rejoice!" This Old Testament counterpart says, "Rejoice ... in everything."

When health goes, it is common for the pleasure capacity to go right along with it. But that does not have to be. Through the power within us we can live above the circumstances of life, no matter how unpalatable those circumstances may be.

Since our joy and rejoicing are to be found in the person of Christ, rather than in our situation or in material things, Satan is hard pressed to rob us of our joy. <u>He cannot take Christ from us</u>! "I am with you always, even to the end of the age," is our Lord's precious promise, and we have never once doubted that.

We may say, "There isn't much we 'put our hand to'

these days." No matter! Life should never be judged by <u>how much</u> we do, but rather by <u>how</u> we do what we do.

Even these times of devotion can be enhanced by the way we put ourselves into them, making them an act of worship as well as a time of gathering the hidden manna. Our Lord is <u>so worthy</u> of praise, and there is <u>so much</u> for which to praise Him. Even in our times of devotion, we are to rejoice before the Lord. That is not a difficult assignment.

"I will bless the Lord at all times: His praise shall continually be in my mouth," will be the attitude with which we approach all our earthly tasks, no matter how small. In the midst of such praise, our souls will be blessed and the natural response will be rejoicing before the Lord.

"... you are to rejoice before the LORD your God in everything you put your hand to."

PATIENT ENDURANCE

*"This calls for <u>patient endurance</u> and <u>faithfulness</u>
on the part of the saints."*   Revelation 13:10c

Let's lift this verse right out of its context and allow it to speak directly to our current situation. A teacher of Hermeneutics would be horrified and see it as a violation of the Scriptures, but it isn't really that. We are not preaching a sermon, interpreting the meaning of this text. We are simply acknowledging that what we are enduring together <u>also</u> calls for patient endurance and faithfulness.

By God's grace and with His help we will be <u>patient</u>, and we will <u>endure</u> this trial in a manner that will be pleasing to Him. We do not enjoy the limitations placed on us, but we do not have to chafe under them, either. Robert McCheyne so eloquently wrote, "You cannot love trouble for its own sake; bitter must always be bitter, and pain must always be pain. God knows you cannot love trouble. Yet for the blessing that it brings, He can make you pray for it."

Patient endurance and faithfulness on the part of the saints are surely very pleasing to God. "Endure hardship ... like a good soldier of Jesus Christ," Paul admonished Timothy. John goes far beyond that here. He asks us to endure <u>patiently</u> and to demonstrate a faithfulness through it all.

We need God's enabling for that kind of gracious response to difficult circumstances. He is giving that enabling and we have reason to rejoice that His grace is indeed sufficient for this trying time. We will serve Him together in whatever ways we can, and leave the scope of that service to His wise determination. We will honor Him by "patient endurance and faithfulness."

MY STRENGTH

"O my <u>Strength</u>, I watch for You; You, O God are my fortress, my loving God. ... I will sing of Your <u>strength</u>, ... I will sing of Your love; You are my fortress, my refuge in times of trouble. O my <u>Strength</u>, I sing praise to You; You O God, are my fortress, my loving God."

Psalm 59

David repeatedly refers to God as his Strength in this Psalm. Saul is out to kill him, and David is putting his trust in God for deliverance from his powerful enemy.

There certainly is an analogy for us here. Satan is not using a person in our situation, but a disease in his attempt to destroy. Our Refuge and Strength is our loving Lord, just as David's was. We gladly take refuge in our Lord, and wait for this storm to be over, content to know that He is a Lord who cares, and we are very safe in that protective, loving care.

David sang praises to his Source of Strength. We follow his example and offer the praise of our hearts to God. Praise comes easily when we reflect upon what we have already experienced of God's faithfulness to us. In so very many ways God has been good to us. He has blessed us wonderfully, and we do not take that for granted.

Our life together has been greatly enriched by being Christians. Our home has had a warmth that only the love of Christ can produce. Our opportunities to serve God have been many and varied, and we have enjoyed serving together. Our trials have been made lighter by being able to cast our cares upon Him. Our needs have been met most graciously year after year. Even in this "time of trouble" God is with us, sustaining us; we are deeply conscious of that and we praise Him for it.

"O my Strength, I watch for You; ... I will sing of Your strength, ... I will sing of Your love; You are my fortress, my refuge in times of trouble. O my Strength, I sing praise to You; You O God, are my fortress, my loving God."

MIGHTY THINGS

"... I fall down on my knees and p. ty ... that out of His glorious, unlimited resources He will give you the mighty inner strengthening of His Holy Spirit." "... I want to remind you that your strength must come from the LORD's mighty power within you."

Ephesians 3:14-16; 6:10 (L.B.)

"Mighty power" and "mighty inner strengthening" are both spoken of in this passage from the Living Bible. It is imperative that we never forget "What a mighty God we serve."

"All power in heaven and on earth is given to Me," was the bold claim the Lord Jesus made, and we know it is true. We have seen that mighty power at work at times. In phenomenal ways we have experienced the outpouring of His mighty workings.

Right now we need Divine strengthening, especially within our spirit, or "inner strengthening" as it is referred to in this passage.

Paul deliberately chose to make more forceful an

already strong statement by use of the word "mighty", so that it becomes a "mighty inner strengthening" and "the Lord's mighty power" within us from which our strength comes.

We have been strengthened for these days. We gladly acknowledge that. God has perfected His own strength in the midst of our physical and emotional weakness, and we marvel to observe it. The normal thing in the midst of our confinement would be for us to chafe and fret, but we have not done that. There is an inner contentment and submission to this radical change of lifestyle that is only explainable on the basis of a mighty inner strengthening by His Holy Spirit. We know well that our strength comes from the Lord's mighty power at work within us, and we are grateful.

"... out of His glorious, unlimited resources He will give you the mighty inner strengthening of His Holy Spirit. ... your strength must come from the LORD's mighty power within you."

LOOK BEYOND

"Let us fix our eyes on Jesus, the author and perfecter of our faith, who for the joy set before Him endured the cross ... Consider Him who endured ... so that you will not grow weary and lose heart."   Hebrews 12:2,3

Jesus looked beyond the intense suffering of the moment and kept His mind fixed upon what was coming later. Looking beyond is an effective way of handling a painful present.

What lies beyond this trial for you? One of two things: either a marvelous testimony of Divine healing that will greatly encourage the faith of others who are struggling, or an even more marvelous personal experience of seeing the culmination of all you have believed through the years. Seeing Jesus, face to face! It is an inconceivable joy.

"It will be worth it all
   When we see Jesus;
      Life's trials will seem so small
         When we see Him."

You <u>will</u> see Him in one way or another, at the end of this trial. You will either see Him in a fabulous Divine intervention, countermanding every prognosis of the physicians, or you will see Him literally.

So then, let us together look beyond the pain, the weakness, the confinement, the medications, the thwarting of plans, and the continuing struggle, to that glorious day when we shall look back upon what we have gone through. We will then remember with joy that He was with us every step of the way to strengthen, help, comfort and enable.

Yes, let's deliberately consider Him who endured, so that we will not grow weary and lose heart.

"Let us fix our eyes on Jesus, the author and perfecter of our faith, who for the joy set before Him endured the cross ... Consider Him who endured ... so that you will not grow weary and lose heart."

LIKE NEW CLOTHES

"How weary we grow of our present bodies. That is why we look forward eagerly to the day when we shall have heavenly bodies which we shall put on like new clothes."

II Corinthians 5:2 (L.B.)

New clothes are undeniably enjoyable to wear. When a garment is new, it actually does something for our spirit! How can we even imagine the exhilaration we shall feel when we put on our heavenly bodies after shedding these worn out, shabby ones?

Yes, we <u>are</u> weary of our present bodies. They have served us for a lot of years now, and though they still do remarkably well when we consider how we have used and abused them, they are obviously showing signs of wear and tear.

The putting on of heavenly bodies may come suddenly for us both as the Lord Jesus returns to catch us up into the air. We don't know all about the schedule of things to come, but we do know that He taught us to expect Him momentarily and made some wonderful promises about that glorious day just around the corner.

Among the exciting prospects surrounding the day of His return is the delight of putting on the "new clothing" of our glorified bodies. We look forward to that marvelous suit for our spirit more than any new dress or suit we have ever bought. The "new clothes" spoken of here will be perfect in every way, <u>eternally</u> perfect, in fact. They will be incapable of weariness. They will never experience pain. They will not age. They will need no sleep to maintain them. They will be very beautiful, with a beauty emanating from the Creator Himself.

It's exciting to contemplate that wonderful day, not far away, when we will put on our long awaited "new clothes."

"How weary we grow of our present bodies. That is why we look forward eagerly to the day when we shall have heavenly bodies which we shall put on like new clothes."

LET US COME BOLDLY

"... Jesus the Son of God is our great High Priest who has gone to heaven itself to help us; therefore <u>let us never stop trusting</u> Him. This High Priest of ours understands our weaknesses, ... So <u>let us come boldly</u> to the very throne of God and <u>stay there</u> to receive His mercy and to find grace to help us in our times of need."

Hebrews 4:14-16 (L.B.)

The writer of Hebrews understands our human tendency to give up after praying and not receiving promptly the full answer to our prayers. He admonishes us: "<u>never stop trusting Him</u>."

He further challenges us to "come boldly to the very throne of God <u>and stay there</u>." That is the audacious position we must take. We must boldly come into the very throne room, <u>and stay there</u>, rather than timorously withdrawing. He is our God - yes, but He is also our Heavenly Father. We can come boldly to our very loving Father with our urgent request for a healing touch, knowing that He loves to respond to His children.

"Never stop trusting," ... "come boldly," ... "stay there," ... "find grace;" these are the admonitions of this passage and we must allow them to permeate our thinking until they deeply affect our spirit and cause our expectations to soar. God has already done wonderful things for us, often above and beyond what man has expected. We have precedent for expectations that go beyond medical prognoses.

Jesus, our High Priest, has gone to Heaven for the express purpose of helping us. We stand before Him asking for help He loves to give. Let's just "stay there" boldly asking for the help we undeniably need in this, our "time of need." Such a firm position is not offensive to God. He has encouraged it!

"... let us never stop trusting Him. let us come boldly to the very throne of God and stay there to receive His mercy and to find grace to help us in our times of need."

I KNOW

"... I know where you stay and when you come and go."   Isaiah 37:28

Here God very succinctly declares His omniscience, and how it affects us. In Psalm 139, David uses sixteen verses to elaborate on this wonderful truth. He lists all the places God sees us, from the moment of conception on - no, even <u>before</u> conception! He makes the statement, "All the days ordained for me were written in your book <u>before one of them came to be</u>." He follows that statement immediately with the words, "How precious to me!" Yes, it <u>is</u> precious to us to realize that God <u>never</u> loses control. It is very meaningful to know that because we are His own, we are <u>never</u> the victims of our circumstances. God knew this day eons ago. He knew the joys we would share. He knew the sorrows. He knew how much strength as well as how much weakness we would have. He knew the proportions of sunshine contrasted with shadow that would comprise this day.

178

With the songwriter we must declare firmly, "Sunshine or shadow, I take them from Thee, knowing Thy grace is sufficient for me."

"I know where you stay, and when you come and go." Lately we have done more staying than we have coming and going. <u>There is nothing wrong with that</u>, as long as it is God-directed, and God planned. We must demonstrate our submission to Him by being:

"Ready to go, ready to stay,
　　Ready our place to fill.
　　　Ready for service, lowly or great,
　　　　Ready to do His will."

Such a complete surrender to the will of God is pleasing to Him. He honors it, and takes pleasure in it. He brings deliverance to those who are pliable in His hands - <u>in His time</u>. Let's rest in the beautiful truth that He knows where we stay, and when or even <u>whether</u> we come and go.

"Praise be to the Lord, to God our Savior, <u>who daily bears</u> our burdens."   Psalm 68:19

What a deep comfort it is to realize that every day - each <u>new</u> day, the Lord lovingly bears our burdens. We think of Him as the Great Burden Bearer, but perhaps have not thought about the fact that He <u>so faithfully</u> continues that ministry to our hearts - day after day after burden-filled day.

I care for your needs daily, and count it a great privilege and joy to be able to serve you, just as I know you would do for me. I don't think of it as a burden, but rather as a privilege and as an opportunity to fulfill commitments I made to you years ago.

His care for us is a fulfillment of promises He made to His beloved as well. "I will never leave you nor forsake you," He promised when we became His children. "I have loved you with an everlasting love," is His own reassurance to our hearts.

We can only marvel that He should love us so, for we

do not see in ourselves anything worth such loving.

"Why should He love me so?
    Why should He love me so?
        Why should my Savior to Calvary go?
        Why should He love me so?"

We sang that often in my home church when I was a
child. It was more than a song to me - it was an
honest question from my amazed young heart.
We don't know why, but we <u>do</u> know that He loves
us dearly and deeply. Out of that great depth of love,
He daily bears our burdens, as He has promised.
Oh, "Praise be to the Lord, to God our Savior, who
<u>daily</u> bears our burdens"!

DESIRES PASS AWAY

"The world and its desires pass away, but the (person) who does the will of God lives forever." I John 2:17

We are increasingly aware that this world and the things in it that have pleased us are steadily losing their luster. There is very little that thrills us or sparks genuine excitement within us anymore.

Most television programs seem to have a ho-hum sameness about them. Food, while not entirely distasteful, is not really enjoyable. Already the world's desires are decidedly passing away.

But the prospect of living forever with renewed energy and a new capacity for enjoyment <u>does</u> interest us greatly. Our youth is to be restored perpetually. Our interest in exploration will return, and we shall have the entire universe to explore. Activities we can no longer enjoy because of physical limitations will become options again. It is a special privilege of the Christian to know that even as his body deteriorates and retreats from abilities once enjoyed, he or she can look forward eagerly to the promised day when this corruptible body puts on immortality, and these weak knees are strengthened. Then our less than perfect hearing will become so fantastically acute that we will be able to distinguish differences in pitch that we never even heard here on earth. For example, God gave us 2000 strings in each of our ear-pianos, but we have only 88 keys on the pianos at church and in our home. That's less than 4 1/2 percent of capability! A great day is ahead of us, a day we can look forward to with genuine excitement.

What is ahead for us far exceeds what we have experienced here. Though "the world and its desires pass away," we can rejoice in the prospect of living forever, because we have done the will of God.

"The world and its desires pass away, but the (person) who does the will of God lives forever."

"Then they came to Elim, where there were twelve springs and seventy palm trees, and they camped there near the water. The whole Israelite community set out from Elim and came to <u>the Desert of Sin</u> ... In the desert the whole community grumbled against Moses and Aaron ... 'You have <u>brought us out into this desert</u> to starve this entire assembly to death.' ... So Moses and Aaron said to all the Israelites, 'In the evening you will know that <u>it was the LORD who brought you out</u> of Egypt, and in the morning you will see the glory of the LORD, because he has heard your grumbling against him ... You will know <u>it was the LORD</u> ... You are not grumbling against us, but against the LORD.'"

Exodus 15:27; 16:1-8

The Israelites complained that Moses and Aaron had brought them into this desert, but they were so very wrong; without question it was the LORD who had done that.

We must <u>never</u> fall into their error. When we enter

one of the "deserts" of life, and are tempted to murmur and complain, we must remember that it was the LORD who brought us into that desert, just as assuredly as on other occasions He has brought us to our Elim with its springs and palm trees.

We <u>love</u> the oasis experiences in life. Springs and palms are exotic and refreshing. We enjoy sitting in the shade of a palm tree and drinking cool water from the spring. But life is not all Elims. There are deserts as well, and we do not want them to be called "The Desert of Sin" in <u>our</u> life.

By God's grace we will recognize and acknowledge that it is the LORD who has led us there. When we find ourselves in a desert, in the midst of our dry spells, we will continue to glorify our Lord, and praise Him even when the hot sand burns our toes.

"... our God ... keeps his covenant of love ..."

Nehemiah 9:32

Oh yes, He does! Indeed He does! We have benefited from His loving faithfulness over and over. How we praise Him!

"I will never leave you nor forsake you" is one of His wonderful promises. We can say with feeling, "He never has!" Through all the difficult terrain we have encountered, God has been there by our side, faithfully guiding our footsteps lest we dash our foot against a stone. He has kept His covenant of love.

"I will instruct you and teach you in the way that you should go," is another of His clear promises. We look back and see specific guidance that is detailed and we are thrilled. Again, He has faithfully kept His covenant of love.

"When you pass through the waters, they will not overflow you, and when you walk through the fire, it will not burn you," He promised us, and though we have been through floods and fire we are still walking in victory, our souls unscathed, even when our bodies have taken a beating. We were not drowned. We were not burned. He has kept His covenant of love. He promised to "supply all (our need) out of His riches in glory by Christ Jesus." Graciously and bountifully He has done that and we have had need of nothing. Even our medical expenses have been so faithfully cared for. He has bountifully kept His covenant of love.

We do not know all that lies ahead of us. It frightens us at times to even think about it. But this we do know, and upon this truth we must continually dwell: Our faithful Lord is One who "keeps His covenant of love." He has in the past - He will in the future, irrespective of what that future includes.

"... our God ... keeps his covenant of love ..."

COMING SOON!

"Behold, I am coming soon!"
"Behold, I am coming soon!"

Revelation 22:7a,12a

Twice in a span of only five verses this announcement is boldly proclaimed. We love to hear this trumpet call echoing from the Revelation Mountain Range.

Only nine verses from the very end of the Bible we come to this twice-stated promise, and it is not the last time the Lord Jesus says it. In the next to the last verse of this final chapter He reaffirms, "Yes, I <u>am</u> coming soon," to which John responds, "Amen. Come quickly, Lord Jesus."

No one who ever lived before us had more reason to expect the fulfillment of that promise than we do. The "signs of His coming multiply; morning light breaks in the eastern sky." We don't have to be experts in Bible prophecy to realize that wars and rumors of wars are a sign of the end times. We have lots of those. Frequent earthquakes will cause the

188

earth to tremble, the Bible predicts. California alone has recently experienced multiplied thousands of them large enough to be recorded on the Richter Scale. Evil will flourish on the earth, the Bible says. The open wickedness is appalling, even in our own country.

What a change the coming of the Lord Jesus will effect! "Satan's dominion will then be o'er; sorrow and sighing shall be no more." The prospect of that painless, sorrowless, sinless day is most appealing. We thrill to read the words of the Lord Jesus that John recorded for us, "Behold, I am coming soon!" It is very easy for us to exclaim along with John, "Amen! Come quickly, Lord Jesus!" To his prayer we add, "And while we wait, please keep that blessed hope burning brightly within us, sustaining and encouraging us greatly."

"Behold, I am coming soon!"
"Behold, I am coming soon!"

A STRENGTHENED FRAME

"The LORD will ... satisfy your needs in a sun-scorched land and will <u>strengthen your frame</u>."   Isaiah 58:11

The Bible is filled with wonderful promises. Those promises are in an entirely different category from the promises we hear the politicians make. God's promises are sure and trustworthy. They are backed by an integrity our world knows little about. He keeps each promise with ease, and has made none of them thoughtlessly.

The satisfying of our needs in a sun-scorched land has a lot of appeal to us right now. We need that. The strengthening of your frame is a very specific need also. Both are promised here. We must believe those promises.

"Standing on the promises of Christ, my King,
  Through eternal ages let His praises ring;
   Glory in the highest I will shout and sing,
   Standing on the promises of God.

Standing on the promises that cannot fail
  When the howling storms of doubt and fear assail,
  By the living word of God I shall prevail,
  Standing on the promises of God.

Standing on the promises I cannot fall,
  Listening every moment to the Spirit's call,
  Resting in my Savior as my all in all,
  Standing on the promises of God."

This verse gives to us two of the thousands of promises upon which we may stand: "The Lord will ... satisfy your needs in a sun-scorched land," and "The Lord ... will strengthen your frame." We need them both and we will claim the fulfillment of them together.

A SIGN

"Turn to me and have mercy on me; grant Your strength to Your servant ... <u>Give me a sign of Your goodness,</u> ... You, O LORD, have helped me and comforted me."   Psalm 86:16,17

"Give me a sign of your goodness." In the King James it reads, "Show me a token for good."

David was wise to ask this of God. He is a God who answers. He is willing to give tokens for good, or signs of His goodness, to those who boldly ask for them.

Let's ask God to give us once again something special that we will easily recognize as a "sign of His goodness." He has throughout this trial given moments of <u>strong</u> encouragement. They have bolstered our faith and have helped us not to cast away our confidence. We need those "tokens."

"You, O Lord have helped me and comforted me," David could say. Almost simultaneously he asked for a sign of God's goodness. So, we do not have to feel as if we are wearying God when we come to Him asking for yet another <u>sign of His goodness</u>.

Let's see what good thing God does for us in the next few days that we can interpret as a <u>sign of His goodness</u>. A spirit of expectation will create a climate in which God can more readily work.

Remembering, then, the ways by which the Lord has already helped and comforted us, we will also be looking for a new <u>sign of His goodness</u> - a token that He intends to do wonderful things in answer to our earnest prayers.

"Turn to me and have mercy on me; grant Your strength to Your servant ... Give me a sign of Your goodness, ... You, O LORD, have helped me and comforted me."

AARON AND HUR

"When Moses ... grew tired, they took a stone and put it under him and he sat on it. Aaron and Hur held his hands up - one on one side, one on the other - so that his hands remained steady till sunset." Exodus 17:12

This account reminds us of those times when we become weary and can no longer do what we need to do by ourselves. That's when we need others to stand by us faithfully, holding our hands up for us.

We have watched friends of ours who have been wondrously sustained in their losses (of spouse, job, position, health, etc.). They have come through the earlier stages of their trials in admirable triumph. Then they reached a point where they were unable to hold their hands steady by themselves any more. They needed others to be praying for them - holding them up faithfully.

That is no sign of weakness, any more than it was a sign of weakness on Moses' part when he could no longer hold up his hands during that battle. It is simply an indication of the limits of human endurance. We can only stand so much stress and strain and then we reach those limits.

In our own current distress there will be times when it becomes difficult for us to pray, simply because we are weary of the battle. You have done so well, <u>so very well</u>, but there must be moments when you are weary of praying, or at least waver in your ability to pray in faith. I falter at times, too. In those moments, it is such a blessing to discover that God has His faithful Aarons and Hurs to be there, holding up our hands through that crisis time of weakness, or weariness, or discouragement. God does not leave us unsupported at that critical juncture.

"When Moses ... grew tired, they took a stone and put it under him and he sat on it. Aaron and Hur held his hands up - one on one side, one on the other - so that his hands remained steady till sunset."

AT OUR RIGHT HAND!

"... He stands at the right hand of the needy one,
to save his life."   Psalm 109:31

In our previous devotional we noted that as Aaron and Hur stood beside Moses and held up his hands, he was sustained in the work he was doing for the Lord that day.   We reminded our own hearts of those "Aarons" and "Hurs" that the Lord has given to us to sustain us. We also acknowledged the privilege we have of responding by standing beside others, like some of our friends, who have recently needed someone to hold up their faltering hands.

Now, here is a verse that, in the light of yesterday's scenario, is very thrilling, for it tells us that one of those who stands by us is the Lord Himself.   The passage even discloses to us which side He is standing on! "... He stands at the right hand of the needy one, to save his life."

God does not use words carelessly. When we couple this promise of a faithful Heavenly Father standing at our right hand, saving your life, with the verse that tells us He holds your right hand, saying to you, "Do not fear," we realize anew that God chooses His words carefully. His position is to your right. His purpose is to spare your life. He has gone on record specifically.

Such literal interpretation of the Bible is scoffed at by those who are worried about fanaticism. The trouble with Christianity, unfortunately, does not seem to be fanaticism, but lethargy. Many people never experience that direct intervention of God in their lives, or at least are unconscious of it when it happens, because they are not trusting for anything, nor looking for anything out of the ordinary. Let's always be alert to the workings of our faithful Lord, and very conscious of His presence at our right hand, holding that hand up when it becomes weary.

"... He stands at the right hand of the needy one, to save his life."

WE CAN

*"He reached down from on high and took hold of me;
He drew me out of deep waters. He rescued me ... You,
O LORD, keep my lamp burning; my God turns my
darkness into light. <u>With Your help I can</u> run through
a barricade; <u>with my God I can</u> scale a wall. As for
God, His way is perfect ..."*   Psalm 18:16-30a

"<u>With Your help I can</u> ..." "<u>With my God I can</u> ..."
Yes, it takes a special enabling of the Lord to be able
to do things now, but that certainly isn't all bad.
When we are strong, it is easy to fall into the error of
doing things in our own strength. When we are
weak, we are forced to call upon <u>His</u> strength for our
activities and then we learn the deeper significance of
the truth that <u>His</u> strength is perfected in <u>our</u>
weakness.

Looking back over the course of this illness, we have
to marvel at the ways the Lord has enabled and
strengthened. There have been <u>so</u> many victories. We
would have loved to have experienced the ultimate

victory of a dramatic and complete healing. To date that has not happened, but there have been a host of smaller victories along the way, and these have glorified the Lord and have encouraged us.

We call them "smaller victories." <u>Are they</u>? The God who sees so many things differently from the way we do may not consider them "smaller." Our learning to lean heavily upon His strength to bring order out of the chaos this disease has wrought may be in His sight a most significant victory. We had our own way of doing things, and it was good, we felt. When things caved in on us, we had to learn to adapt and to depend wholly upon Him to lead us through the darkness. He has done that. We can do all things through Christ who strengthens us - yes, <u>with His help</u> we can!

"You, O LORD, keep my lamp burning; my God turns my darkness into light. With Your help I can run through a barricade; with my God I can scale a wall. As for God, His way is perfect."

WEAKNESS, HOPE

"He does not crush the weak, nor quench the smallest hope ..." Matthew 12:20 (L.B.)

Quite the contrary! Our Lord Jesus perfects His strength in the midst of our weakness, strengthening our weak knees, and enabling us to accomplish what we could not, without His help. He encouraged hope with wonderful promises, and beautiful examples of His loving nature as He healed one after another. Then, we were reminded that He is the same today as He was yesterday, and will be forever.

Both weakness <u>and</u> hope must be a part of the scene for us right now. One through no choice of our own, but the other through deliberate choice. We do <u>not</u> choose weakness. That is thrust upon us. We <u>can</u> choose to hope, and this we will not relinquish without a noteworthy fight.

"He does not crush the weak." It is the nature of the Lord Jesus to assist the weak, lovingly. When we think of what He has brought you through, we marvel. The various medical procedures have taken their toll and at times have left you with precious little human strength remaining. Then the Lord has come to you and renewed your strength, time and time again. The prognoses of the doctors have been incorrect so many times. That in itself is faith building, and a help in those times when the enemy attempts to destroy <u>all</u> our faith through unwelcome developments.

Our smallest hopes are encouraged by the Lord Jesus. They are given foundation by promises that came from His own lips. Let's recall a few of them. "I will never leave you nor forsake you." "As your days, so shall your strength be." "If you shall ask anything in My name, that I will do that the Father may be glorified in the Son." "My grace is sufficient for you." Oh yes, it's true: *"He does not crush the weak, nor quench the smallest hope"!*

WAIT QUIETLY

"The LORD is my portion; therefore I will wait for Him. The LORD is good to those whose hope is in Him, to the one who seeks Him; it is good to wait quietly for the salvation of the LORD."

Lamentations 3:24-26

We are not good at waiting. Too much waiting makes us fidgety. We live in a microwave, instant-potatoes, fast-food, fax machine, nano-second world. It even irritates us that our computer doesn't bring up the thing we ask for more quickly, and we look forward to the new generations of computers that will be one hundred times faster than the current ones.

We always seem to choose the slowest line, whether it is at the bank or in Mac Donald's. We hate being put on hold while someone tends to an incoming phone call on their abominable "call-waiting" modern convenience. We detest it when the clerk who is at last taking care of us answers the phone and treats that person as if he has a perfect right to cut in line ahead of us, as long as he uses the telephone to do it.

So now, we are told to "wait quietly." There is another text that tells us to "wait patiently." Strong's concordance lists more than three dozen times that the word "patient" in one form or another is used! In Hebrews 10:36 we read, "you have need of patience." It's true! Waiting, and especially waiting quietly, does not come easily nor normally to us. We have prayed long for deliverance, and have waited for an absolute and outright miracle. We have enjoyed mini-miracles that have greatly glorified God and deeply blessed us, but we still await the big one. "Mercy drops 'round us are falling, but for the showers we plead!" God hears that pleading, and will respond in His time.

"The LORD is my portion; therefore I will wait for Him. The LORD is good to those whose hope is in Him, to the one who seeks Him; it is good to wait quietly for the salvation of the LORD."

TRANSCENDENT PEACE

"... the peace of God, which transcen ls all understanding,
will guard your hearts and your minds in Christ Jesus."

Philippians 4:7

What a blessing transcendent peace is! There are times
when peace does not come naturally, in fact it is
downright unnatural, yet God provides a sweet,
beautiful peace that the world can only marvel at.
Two hymns eloquently speak of the transcendent
peace of God:

"Far away in the depths of my spirit tonight
  Rolls a melody sweeter than psalm;
In celestial-like strains it unceasingly falls
  O'er my soul like an infinite calm.

What a treasure I have in this wonderful peace
  Buried deep in the heart of my soul,
So secure that no power can mine it away
  While the years of eternity roll!

I am resting tonight in this wonderful peace,
  Resting sweetly in Jesus' control;
For I'm kept from all danger by night and by day
  And His glory is flooding my soul!

Peace, peace, wonderful peace,
　　Coming down from the Father above!
Sweep over my spirit forever, I pray,
　　In fathomless billows of love!"

It is indeed a peace that transcends all understanding, and the question and answer aspect of this other hymn reflects the wonder of it all:

"Peace, perfect peace, in this dark world of sin?
　　... The blood of Jesus whispers "peace" within.
Peace, perfect peace, with sorrows surging 'round?
　　... On Jesus' bosom naught but calm is found.
Peace, perfect peace, with loved ones far away?
　　... In Jesus' keeping we are safe, and they.
Peace, perfect peace, our future all unknown?
　　... Jesus we know, and He is on the throne.
Peace, perfect peace, death shadowing us and ours?
　　... Jesus has vanquished death and all its powers."

Yes, the peace of God is a peace that transcends all understanding - transcendent peace!　　*

THIS IS THE DAY!

"This is the day the LORD has made. We will rejoice and be glad in it."   Psalm 118:24 (L.B.)

We read this together at the close of the day, when its events are indelibly etched upon the historical page, never to be altered.

But, whether it has been a wonderfully pain-free day, with great encouragements to our faith and accomplishments that give us warm feelings of satisfaction, or one in which the struggle with pain and weakness was burdensome, it still has been "the day that the Lord has made." We can "rejoice and be glad in it."

"Sunshine or shadow" - we take them from Him. Bane or blessing, we sense His presence with us, regardless. Victory or apparent defeat - we can still be confident, for we know that there is no real defeat to the Christian whose life is totally committed to the Life-Giver.

Yes, this day, and every other day is a day the Lord

has made and we will not give the enemy the satisfaction of controlling the attitudes we hold in connection with it. We <u>will</u>, with holy determination, "rejoice and be glad in it"!

We look back over this storm-filled segment of our life together. The storm began dramatically when a few words from the mouth of a doctor changed the fiber of earthly existence for us drastically. Yet we recognize that our Lord has been very faithful in walking with us through this stormy time, just as He was in our brighter, clearer days.

So much has changed, but Jesus? ...never! Glory to His Name! It is very true that "<u>All</u> may change, but Jesus never!" He is "the same yesterday and today and forever." No wonder we rejoice!

"This is the day the LORD has made. We will rejoice and be glad in it."

EVENING AND MORNING

"And there was evening, and there was morning - the first day." "And there was evening, and there was morning - the second day." "And there was evening, and there was morning - the third day." Genesis 1:5b ff

This unfamiliar way of counting days proceeds throughout the first chapter of Genesis very consistently: "And there was evening, and there was morning..." right on through the sixth day. So, all the working days of creation are described putting the "evening" word first. We would have said, "There was morning and there was evening - the first day," etc. We talk of the springtime of life, and the final years of our lives we call "autumn," phasing on into the "winter." (... of our discontent!)

God's way of looking at things is refreshingly different. When we see our lives winding down, with "evening" having come upon us, God says that our "evening" is nearly over, and soon our "morning" will be arriving.

The chorus-writer captured the essence of this when he penned the words:

"Some golden <u>daybreak</u>, Jesus will come.
  Some golden <u>daybreak</u>, victories all won.
    He'll shout the vict'ry, break through the blue,
      Some golden <u>daybreak</u>, for me - for you."

Yes, it is to be the dawning of a new day, rather than the conclusion of an old one. That songwriter chose his words well.

God's perspective on almost everything is so different from our own and <u>so</u> much better. Let's capture some of the excitement of looking upon this time of life as the beginning of new and wondrous things, rather than as our "autumn" or even "winter." Let the prospect of an eternal springtime for our souls burn brightly within us. Evening <u>physically</u>, yes, but <u>morning</u> spiritually. *"And there was evening, and (then) there was morning."*

AS GOLD

"... He knows the way that I take; when He has tested me, I will come forth <u>as gold</u>."   Job 23:10

Yes, He knows the way that we take. "Jesus knows, and best of all He cares, and I belong to Him!" the songwriter exclaimed. It's true, "Nobody knows de trouble I seen; nobody knows but Jesus," (as the old Negro Spiritual insists). It is very comforting to remind our hearts that "He knows the way that (we) take."

Job follows that statement of fact with the assurance that "When He has tested me, I will come forth <u>as gold</u>." Job saw the testing as a refining fire that consumed the dross and made him presentable to God as refined gold.

This time of testing is temporary, no matter what the final outcome may be. In any eventuality there will be a coming forth and it shall be as gold coming out of the fire. May the Lord Jesus be very pleased with all that is accomplished in this fire. May we be so submissive to Him and so sensitive to His instructions that in a special kind of way these will be precious days to us, and <u>to Him as well</u>!

There are frustrations in being confined, but along with Madam Guyon who wrote of being "a little bird ... shut in from fields of air," we too, in our temporary cage shall "sit and sing of Him who placed us there." We will refuse to chafe, and will take each new day as something fresh from His loving hand, just as we did in the days when we were both ambulatory and came and went as we planned and pleased.

There is something very positive and upbeat about these assuring words, "<u>I will come forth</u>." We look forward together to the time of victorious forthcoming spoken of here.

"... He knows the way that I take; when He has tested me, I will come forth as gold."

WORTH MORE

"Are not five sparrows sold for two pennies? Yet not one of them is forgotten by God. Indeed, the very hairs of your head are all numbered. Don't be afraid; you are worth more than many sparrows."   Luke 12:6,7

How much are you worth to me? How much am I worth to you? We cannot answer that question, for no price can be put on the love we have for each other, nor on how much we mean to each other. That cannot be measured monetarily.

God's eye is on the sparrow, and He knows when it falls. Not one of them is ever forgotten by God. How amazing! It speaks volumes about what He thinks of us, and the way He cares for us.

"Worth more than many sparrows" - the comparison is so extreme that the point is forcefully made. We are worth ever so much more than sparrows to God, and if He watches over every one of them, He surely watches over you and me. Let's take great comfort in this beautiful truth.

God's watchful care over us has been demonstrated so beautifully at times that we have become in those moments strongly conscious of it. At other times we do not have that consciousness at all, but it doesn't change anything except our own spirit. We can be needlessly concerned or even depressed when we lose sight of the extent of His loving care. Our enemy would love to rob us of the sweet consciousness of being in His wondrous care. We must discipline our minds to think positively even when circumstances are negative and symptoms persist in raising their ugly heads.

We are God's dearly loved "more-than-sparrows," and can revel in that truth even on the darkest of days. God doesn't have trouble seeing in darkness like we do.

"Don't be afraid; you are worth more than many sparrows."

"Then the princes, governors, captains, and counselors crowded around them and saw that the fire hadn't touched them - not a hair of their heads was singed; their coats were unscorched, and they didn't even smell of smoke!"   Daniel 3:27 (L.B.)

The longer we spend together in this furnace of affliction, the greater the danger that the smell of smoke will cling to us. We can deliberately avoid that.

By God's grace we can keep fresh spiritually and can even be a blessing to those who come by to see us, or who minister to us in various ways. The grace of God is being demonstrated to those who know the length of this trial, as they see us in victory, rather than bemoaning the duration of the distress.

The words, "My grace is sufficient for you" are as true and applicable today as they were back when we first needed them so badly. His grace has no measure! That brings those comforting lyrics to mind again:

"When we have exhausted our store of endurance,
 When our strength has failed ere the day is half done,
  When we reach the end of our hoarded resources,
   Our Father's full giving is only begun.

His love has no limit, His grace has no measure,
 His power has no boundary known unto men;
  For out of His infinite riches in Jesus,
   He giveth, and giveth, and giveth again!"

Annie Johnson Flint

With this kind of boundless provision, we are able to remain in the furnace until He brings us out, and then to come forth still smelling fresh as a summer breeze and as fragrant as the honeysuckle.

"... the fire hadn't touched them - not a hair of their heads was singed; their coats were unscorched, and they didn't even smell of smoke!"

PRESS ON!

"... one thing I do: Forgetting what is behind and straining toward what is ahead, <u>I press on</u> toward the goal to win the prize for which God has called me heavenward in Christ Jesus."   Philippians 3:13,14

"Here are the words of the anthem the choir is singing tomorrow," June Smith, from Shell Point Village in Florida wrote:

"When the valley is deep.

When the mountain is steep,

When the body is weary,

When we stumble and fall;

When the choices are hard,

When we're battered and scarred,

When we've spent our resources,

When we've given our all...

In Jesus' name <u>we press on</u>!

Dear Lord, with the prize

Clear before our eyes,

<u>We</u> find the strength to <u>press on</u>."

Yes, we press on toward the goal to win the prize, and when the prize is clear before our eyes, "we find the strength to press on."

Most of earth's enjoyments have been taken from us at this point. We cannot travel together. We cannot eat out together. We cannot sit in church together. We cannot vacation together.

But we can pray together. We can talk together. We can rejoice together. We can cry together. We can still be together, and for two who care so much about each other, that is one of the greatest joys of all.

It may take some straining and pressing, as Paul admits here, but together, in Jesus' Name, we will press on. Yes, "straining toward what is ahead (we will) press on toward the goal to win the prize for which God has called us heavenward in Christ Jesus."

To order additional copies of **HIDDEN MANNA**, please complete the following:

Ship to: (please print)
Name _____
Address _____
City, State, Zip _____
Home Telephone: ( ) _____ - _____

1 copy of **HIDDEN MANNA**	$ 8.00	$ _____	
2 copies for	$15.00	$ _____	
___ copies (3 or more) each	$ 7.00	$ _____	
Tennessee residents add 8.25% tax		$ _____	

Total payment enclosed: $ _____

Make checks payable to:
Mail to: ....   **CHARLES SHEPSON**
1405 Sundial Ct.
Fort Myers, FL 33908

- -

To order additional copies of **HIDDEN MANNA**, please complete the following:

Ship to: (please print)
Name _____
Address _____
City, State, Zip _____
Home Telephone: ( ) _____ - _____

1 copy of **HIDDEN MANNA**	$ 8.00	$ _____	
2 copies for	$15.00	$ _____	
___ copies (3 or more) each	$ 7.00	$ _____	
Tennessee residents add 8.25% tax		$ _____	

Total payment enclosed: $ _____

Make checks payable to:
Mail to: ....   **CHARLES SHEPSON**
1405 Sundial Ct.
Fort Myers, FL 33908